DISASTER IN DEARBORN

DISASTER

IN DEARBORN

The Story of the Edsel

Thomas E. Bonsall

STANFORD GENERAL BOOKS
An Imprint of Stanford University Press
Stanford, California 2002

Stanford University Press
Stanford, California

Printed in the United States of America
on acid-free, archival-quality paper.

Library of Congress Cataloging-in-Publication Data

Bonsall, Thomas E.
   Disaster in Dearborn : the story of the Edsel / Thomas E. Bonsall.
     p.   cm.
   Includes bibliographical references and index.
   ISBN 0-8047-4654-0 (cloth : alk. paper)
   1. Edsel automobile—History. 2. Ford Motor Company—
Decision making. 3. Product management. I. Title.
TL215.E37 B66   2002
629.222'2—dc21   2002009080

Original Printing 2002

Last figure below indicates year of this printing:
11 10 09 08 07 06 05 04 03 02

Designed by James P. Brommer
Typeset in 11/15 Garamond

Acknowledgments

The author is indebted to numerous individuals and organizations who have assisted the research that went into this book. The individuals listed below are in the positions they occupied when their assistance was offered. Since this book was "in process" for twenty years, many of them have moved on, and three, at least, are deceased. The author extends sincere apologies to anyone inadvertently omitted.

Those who assisted with the research that went into the text included Ed Gorman, Lincoln-Mercury's public relations manager when the original research was undertaken in 1980. He died prior even to the completion of that research, but this book benefits mightily from his long-ago support. Roy Brown, Jr., Bob Jones, and Gary Griffiths, all original Edsel designers, exhibited great patience during lengthy interviews with the author and with Robert Weenick. Richard Stout, a former member of the product planning staff at the Mercury-Edsel-Lincoln Division, not only submitted to several interviews, but took the time to proof the manuscript and offer numerous helpful suggestions and comments. Edsel restorers Charlie Wells, and Leland and John Hardy also supplied valuable information.

Those who assisted with the photo research included Robert Weenick and, again, Roy Brown, the original chief designer of the Edsel design studio, who made his personal scrapbook of Edsel design development sketches and photos available. Jack Telnack, Bill Boyer, Bill Harris, Steffie Hovious, Dennis Paperd, Ken Wagel, all of the Ford Motor Company Design Center, assisted in making Design Center photos available. Those who proved helpful in making other Ford Motor Company photography available included Darelen Flaterly, with the Ford Motor Company Industrial Archives, and Bill Buffa, with Ford Motor Company Photomedia.

Other Ford Motor Company personnel whose assistance defies categorization, but was no less important, included Stan Cousino, with Ford Motor Company Public Relations; Rita Cronin; Dave Doman; T. J. Feahney; John Jasmer; John Menning; Bill Nagel; Harley Selling; and Bill Rigstad.

Contents

DISASTER IN DEARBORN

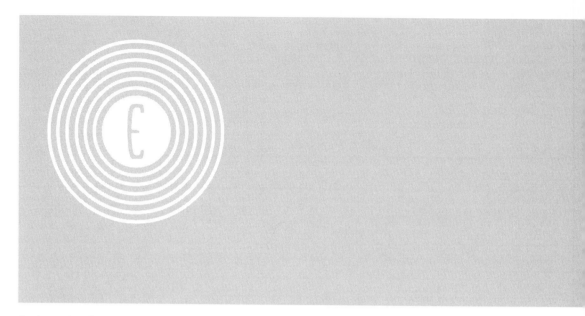

At the national press preview, a 1958 Edsel Citation with Ford brothers. *Left to right*, William Clay, Benson, and Henry II.

Introduction

THIS IS A STORY that has continued to fascinate people as few other epic disasters in modern history. Certainly few cars have grabbed the public's fancy as much as the ill-fated Edsel—the Titanic of automobiles, a marketing disaster whose magnitude has made it a household word. Indeed, for a parallel one must go back to the Titanic itself, which sank in 1912. Both have become metaphors for overweening management ambition and shortsightedness—or worse.

Like the Titanic, however, the true nature of the Edsel disaster is poorly understood and likely to be seen in overly simplified terms. All those people died on the Titanic because there weren't enough lifeboats to go around, or so goes the common wisdom. The Edsel, we are told, failed because it was ugly, or because Ford Motor Company relied too heavily on motivational research. In fact, there were a dozen serious errors that contributed to the Titanic calamity, the shortage of lifeboats being perhaps the least of them. A few years ago I wrote a book on the subject—*Titanic, The Story of the Great White Star Line Trio: The Olympic, the Titanic and the Britannic*, now out of print—that examined the subject in detail. There was even a major element of bad luck. So it was with the Edsel. Including bad luck, a conspiracy of factors bedeviled the Edsel project, while the most popular explanations—the styling and the motivational research—may have been the least of them, if, indeed, they were factors at all.

Believe it or not, there were (and are) people who liked the looks of the Edsel, this writer included. I can still vividly remember my first ride in an Edsel a couple of days before the official announcement in September, 1957. A man named Harry Putt, who had formerly worked for my father, had signed on as a salesman at Ralph May's Edsel dealership in Kent, Ohio. My father went up to see him, taking me in tow, and the two of us were given a hush-hush pre-announcement test drive. The car was a large, Mercury-bodied Citation—and what an impressive-looking machine it was. As a young collector of car catalogs, I had often pressed my parents into taking me around to the car dealerships, and there must have been many similar experiences, but that Edsel ride is one of the few I can still remember with any clarity. Forty-four years later I am still impressed by that car.

The Edsel, for good or for ill, maintains a remarkable hold on the popular imagination. After a time span that has included several wars and assassinations, repeated fuel shocks and bruising recessions—even astounding acts of terrorism—it is difficult to explain this. The Edsel was not even close to being the worst business calamity of all time, or even the worst in the history of the auto industry. The Chrysler Airflow debacle in 1934 was at least as terrible a failure (and was very nearly as celebrated at the time), while the Lockheed R-1011 engine program bankrupted Rolls-Royce. The 1938 Graham—which the company called the "Spirit of Motion," but which everyone else called the "sharknose"—destroyed that company as a viable auto producer. Despite their good looks, the famed 1953 Studebakers—which are fondly remembered for their Raymond Loewy styling—arguably did the same to Studebaker. The Edsel wasn't even necessarily the worst product failure suffered by Ford Motor Company. The inflammable Pinto in the 1970s and the Explorer in recent times probably resulted in far more real damage to the firm than did the notorious Edsel. Yet, the Pinto is almost forgotten today and the Explorer doubtless will be in time.

The reason for the enduring popular fascination with the Edsel is the same as with the Titanic. People are mesmerized by the mighty brought low. Throughout history writers have produced a steady stream of morality plays in various guises dealing with the impudence of man constantly trying to go places he was never—whether by fate or by the deity—meant to go, trying to do things he was never meant to do. The Titanic became a modern morality play. Man had reached too far, gotten too arrogant, and had, inevitably, been given a comeuppance. So it was with the Edsel. The Edsel was supposed to be the great triumph of the Ford Motor Company and its modern marketing acumen, the car that would catapult Ford to equal status with General Motors, but which came to serve a larger function as a metaphor for the hubris of Detroit, in general.

Amazingly, given the foregoing, there has never been an important Edsel book. Quite apart from the broader implications of the story, there has never even been a narrowly defined automotive history that covered the product, how it was created, how and what was produced. This book should fill both voids. It is the result of years of research, including access to the Ford Design Center archives which unearthed some remarkable material without which the full design story would remain forever untold. Many of the key original Edsel design team stylists were interviewed and some have supplied additional archival material. The result is a unique and important treatment of the car from its first sketches in 1955 to the last, unlamented 1960 models.

My own serious interest in an Edsel book began to take root as early as 1980. I had occasion to do research into the Edsel at the time I researched my Lincoln history, The Lincoln Motorcar, and a projected companion volume on Mercury. Prior to my Lincoln research, I did not know that Edsel had been part of the same marketing division as Mercury and Lincoln, and was surprised (to say the least) to discover important Edsel material buried in the dark recesses of the Lincoln-Mercury Division historical files. I was further amazed and excited by the design photos subsequently unearthed. Eventually, it seemed appropriate to plan a trilogy to include all of the major nameplates in the Mercury-Edsel-Lincoln (M-E-L) Division. The Mercury volume remains a pipe dream, but the Edsel story is related in these pages.

One of the truths in writing automotive histories is that there are nearly as many views regarding how any given subject should be approached as there are writers interested in that given subject. The way this book has been organized was given a great deal of thought. Not content to describe the product and its development, this book goes further and tries to explain why the Edsel program was begun in the first place and, of equal importance, what went wrong. As a result, the story related herein may cover a lot more ground than many readers would expect.

The opening chapters, for example, cover the life of the Edsel's namesake: Edsel Bryant Ford, who died in 1943. The reader will be struck by the hopelessness of his position with regard to Ford Motor Company. He and a few others (sales manager, Jack Davis, for one) understood with crystal clarity what was happening to the company, but were almost powerless to do anything about it. This was a nightmare in the classic sense. To return to the analogy of the Titanic, it must have been rather like standing on the bridge, seeing the iceberg dead ahead, and being unable to communicate the imminent disaster to the officer at the helm.

The third chapter deals with the development of the automobile industry in America, and of the medium-priced field, in particular, in the years leading up to the beginning of Ford Motor Company's resurgence at the end of World War II. To some, this may seem a curious way to begin a book ostensibly about a product built in the late 1950s. It is, however, the only way to tell the full Edsel story, for the Edsel story is about much more than a car.

The Edsel program was a deadly serious corporate undertaking designed to help remedy years of mismanagement at Ford Motor Company. Beginning in the 1920s, the highest growth and lushest profits in the auto industry were to be found in the burgeoning medium-priced field. Henry Ford stubbornly ignored this development—and a lot of other things besides, including the rare talents of his remarkable son—and, in the process, nearly brought about the collapse of his company as a serious auto producer. The story of Ford Motor Company in the first two decades of the reign of Henry II is the story of the massive effort undertaken to regain the momentum that had been cast away and return the company to a position of leadership in the industry. The Edsel program was the most spectacular failure in that effort. The Edsel cannot be properly understood, however, without understanding how Ford Motor Company nearly came to ruin in the first place and how it sought to regain the ground that had been lost. To put it another way, the Edsel was but a pawn in a complex, high-stakes chess game, and cannot be understood without also understanding the game of which it was a part.

Particular attention has been given to the internal politics of Ford Motor Company at the time. Back then, Ford was the most "political" of the car companies, with well-entrenched factions vying daily for control. A key reason for the ultimate failure of the Edsel program was the corrosive effect upon it by the intramural warfare between these factions. Of course, most of this was unintentional; no one within the company wanted a major disaster. Today, we would call it collateral damage but the cumulative effect was devastating.

Finally, the Edsel product itself is comprehensively covered, and there will be many surprises in that regard, even for Edsel enthusiasts. The Ford Design Center photos will prove to be a revelation to most readers, even to those who already know something about the designing of the Edsel. The little-known Edsel Comet program is included, a car subsequently produced as a Mercury. Few are aware that the initial 1960 Ford and Edsel cars were to have been reworked off the 1959 body shell. At the last minute, those cars were scrapped and an entirely new 1960 body shell was rushed to completion. This book contains the design development of both 1960 Edsels and reveals the reason for the staggeringly expensive about-face. Moreover, the 1959 Mercury-based Edsels (which also were fully designed, then scrapped at the last minute) are also included.

This book should prove instructive in many ways not only to dyed-in-the-wool Edsel enthusiasts, but to anyone interested in the history of American business. The Edsel program was a colossal disaster that holds many important lessons for us today.

CHAPTER ONE

Henry and Edsel in a 1905 Model F.

Edsel Ford: The Early Years

EDSEL IS THE FORGOTTEN FORD, a man almost completely overshadowed by his famous father, Henry Ford I, and his almost equally celebrated son, Henry Ford II. When *Automotive News*, the auto industry trade newspaper, published its Ford 75th Anniversary special issue in 1978, included were feature articles on all the other key family figures in Ford Motor Company history. Even Edsel II, Edsel's grandson, got splashy treatment. But, for Edsel I, there were just casual mentions in passing scattered throughout the issue. It wasn't that Edsel Ford was exactly ignored, but there was a notable lack of the sort of attention lavished on the other key Ford men throughout the company's history.

In a sense, this is understandable. It is not easy being the son of a legend, especially when you are retiring and publicity-shy. Still, Edsel served as president of Ford Motor Company for nearly a quarter of a century. Although largely a figurehead in the organizational sense—and in the sense that an organization even existed at Ford Motor Company in those days—he nevertheless managed to influence or direct key decisions that changed the course of Ford Motor Company in dramatic ways.

Still, Edsel Ford's life was not an easy one. It is generally accepted that

Henry Ford was a mean-spirited, narrow-minded man who despised his son and eventually destroyed him by a refusal to love or nurture him. There is enough truth in this to make it impossible to dismiss completely, and the stories were certainly legion:

- Henry Ford angrily shouting, "Edsel, you shut up!" and storming out of an executive luncheon at which Edsel had had the temerity to suggest the need for modern, hydraulic brakes.[1]

- Henry Ford, on occasions too numerous to mention, countermanding Edsel's orders and summarily firing executives closest to him.

- Henry Ford refusing to acknowledge his son's desperate condition even as he lay dying of stomach cancer, blaming it all on Edsel's high-society lifestyle.

Yet, there was another side to Henry Ford. He could be tolerant, even generous. He loved his son, by all accounts of those who knew him well. And, Edsel loved him in return and, perhaps more important, was completely loyal. As the elder Ford got on in years, though, he became more and more rigid in his ways and more and more of a torment to those around him, Edsel included.

The essential problem, from Edsel's perspective, was that he possessed a basically different personality from his father. He was an introverted man who disliked confrontation, and especially disliked confrontations with his father. He was sensitive, while his father was all-too-often insensitive, even cruel. He was cultured and elegant, in contrast to his father's rough-hewn, even primitive, tastes. He was highly creative and artistic, whereas his father had little artistic sense and let others do most of his creative thinking. The two of them could have made a remarkable team. Unfortunately, the father never seemed to grasp the fact that his son's differences were a strength, not a failing. Where Edsel was gentle, Henry saw weakness. Where Edsel was imaginative, Henry saw frivolousness. Henry spent years trying to make Edsel into a carbon copy of himself instead of letting Edsel be his own man.

Edsel was the only child of Henry and Clara Bryant Ford. The name "Edsel" comes from Hebrew and means "from the wealthy man's hall," although it is doubtful the thirty-year-old Henry knew that. He and his wife of five years had just moved to Detroit from the nearby Michigan countryside. Henry was to be employed as an electrical "engineer" with the Detroit Edison Company. In reality, he was little more than a glorified, if gifted, mechanic.

If ever there was a man born to the auto industry, it had to have been Edsel Ford. He came into the world on November 6, 1893, a little more than a

Clara Bryant Ford.

month before his father began work on his first two-cycle engine. Two-and-a-half years later, little Edsel got his first ride in an automobile, the first Ford "quadricycle." Henry Ford was on his way. It would take several more years and several different companies before he finally struck it big, but his—and Edsel's—futures were cast.

In 1899, when Edsel was six, his father's first automotive venture—the Detroit Automobile Company—was organized, but never really got off the ground. Probably, fewer than a dozen vehicles were built. On November, 20, 1901, the company was reorganized at the behest of the investors and given the name of the Henry Ford Company. Ford was given a one-sixth interest, but he had wanted a 25–30 percent interest and chafed under what he considered to be his inadequate share in the profits. The last straw for Ford was when Henry M. Leland was brought in as an outside advisor to oversee development of the new model, i.e., to supervise Ford. The situation deteriorated rapidly on both sides and the inevitable break came on March 12, 1902. Ford was given $900 and an agreement that the company would cease to use his name.

Ford turned to racing in 1902—but only long enough to secure a new backer for passenger car production: a prosperous coal merchant named Alexander Malcomson.[2] On June 16, 1903, the Ford Motor Company was at last incorporated. There were twelve stockholders and Ford's share was 25.5 percent. The new company grew rapidly, especially following the introduction of the Model T in 1908.

The young Edsel deserves indirect credit for the introduction of mass production at Ford Motor Company in 1911–13. Clarence W. Avery was a supervisor of manual training at the Detroit University School where Edsel was a

Edsel Bryant Ford, 1916.

student, and Edsel introduced him to the elder Ford. Before long, Avery found himself on the payroll at the giant Ford plant at Highland Park. Avery was the most important theoretical influence behind mass production at Ford Motor Company, just as Charles E. Sorensen, Henry Ford's manufacturing genius, was the most important person with regard to actually putting it into practice.

Although Detroit University School was a college preparatory school, Edsel never attended a college or university. He went to work for Ford Motor Company in 1912 when he was nineteen and remained on the payroll until the day he died more than thirty years later.

Somewhere along the line, Edsel discovered that he liked designing cars more than he liked tinkering with them mechanically, and he began to keep a scrapbook of automotive styling. He would clip pictures of cars that intrigued him, and even circle the features that he liked best. This scrapbook, which survives in the Ford Archives, indicates unmistakably that his early preference was for big, luxurious cars—not at all the sort his father built.

Nor was Edsel's developing interest purely academic. When he was sixteen, in 1909, he built a speedster to his own design for personal transportation, and thus began a series of custom cars built by or for him for his own use, culminating thirty years later in the legendary first Continental. In the 1920s, his tastes ran to custom-bodied creations on the Lincoln chassis. By the 1930s, he seemed to prefer Ford-based sports cars and, occasionally, European exotics.

Neighbors recalled that he drove a bright yellow Stutz Bearcat around the

Eleanor Clay Ford, circa 1916.

time he courted and won Eleanor Clay. They were wed in 1916. She was a niece of Joseph L. Hudson, the Detroit department store magnate for whom the Hudson car was named, and her father, William Clay, had managed the store. Following his death in 1908, she and her mother moved into Hudson's home, and, following his death in 1912, continued to live there. At the time of her wedding with Edsel, the newspapers depicted the union as one of money marrying society, with the nouveau riche Fords obviously supplying the money. While the Hudson family may have been considered more socially established than the Fords, though, they were certainly no strangers to affluence.

Edsel was named president of Ford Motor Company on January 1, 1919, at the ripe old age of twenty-five. His sudden elevation was part of a hoax his father perpetrated on the non-family stockholders to force them to sell. Henry claimed he was leaving the company to start another enterprise that would produce a radical new car of his own design, and in that way depressed the value of the stock he intended to buy. Edsel remained in the titular control even after the company was reorganized, but Henry and Sorensen made nearly all the important decisions.

So, Edsel became the proverbial bird in the gilded cage. He was president of one of the largest industrial organizations in the world at a stage in life when most men are just starting their careers, but the position meant nothing. If anything, it was worse than nothing, because it tended to isolate him and make it even more difficult for him to project his own unique personality.

It was perhaps out of frustration that Edsel acted to persuade his father to purchase the faltering Lincoln Motor Company in the early months of 1922. Quite possibly, he saw the Lincoln company as a place outside his father's interest where he could exercise some real authority on his own. Whatever the motivation, Edsel was destined to play a central role in the development of the Lincoln.

Back when Henry Ford left the Henry Ford Company in 1902 with $900 and his name, the investors had implored Henry Leland and his son Wilfred to remain on to run the operation. Although at first reluctant, Leland finally agreed to do so—and the Cadillac Automobile Company was born. Eventually, the Lelands sold out to General Motors, then had a falling out with William C. Durant over the subject of war production. It was 1917, America was just entering World War I, and the Lelands wanted to assist the War Department in production of aircraft engines. According to the Leland version of the story, Durant, a pacifist, refused, and so Henry and Wilfred Leland resigned in protest. C. S. Mott, a General Motors director at the time, insisted years later that they had been fired for insubordination. In any event, the Lelands were gone forever from General Motors and formed another company to produce aircraft engines: The Lincoln Motor Company, named for the elder Leland's hero, Abraham Lincoln.

After the war, Henry Leland and his team set about doing what they did best: building quality cars. The Lincoln Motor Car Company and the Lincoln "L-Series" automobile resulted. The L-Series was Henry Leland's masterpiece and incorporated two decades of expertise from what was one of the finest car-building teams in the world. Indeed, the L-Series was arguably the most advanced car of its type built anywhere at the time of its introduction in 1921. Every L-Series car prior to the Ford takeover bore the phrase "Leland-built" on its radiator shell, and it was a phrase that meant a great deal when fine cars were discussed. In fact, the fabled Leland quality was its biggest selling point.

The one shortcoming of the L-Series was its appearance. Henry M. Leland, like Henry Ford and many other industry pioneers, had little natural aesthetic sense and saw no need to acquire one. To be fair, in the early years of the industry—when the first question a prospect asked was, "will it run?" —aesthetics were a minor issue. As the automobile approached its maturity, however, buyers turned their attention to other matters, such as comfort and beauty. Even by the unexciting design standards of 1921, the L-Series was remarkably dowdy. All of this might have been of little consequence—and the Lelands quickly realized the problem and were moving to address it—but a sharp economic recession unexpectedly made the issue moot.

The changing of the guard at Lincoln, February 1922. *Standing, left to right,* Henry Ford and Henry Leland; *seated, left to right,* Edsel Ford and Wilfred Leland.

Unfortunately, there could not have been a worse time than 1921 to introduce a new nameplate. As the economy worsened, even established makes such as Pierce-Arrow teetered on the brink, while General Motors only narrowly escaped catastrophe. Even giant Ford Motor Company had a few unsettled moments. In that environment, the Lincoln Motor Car Company slid toward bankruptcy before it really had a chance. It looked as if Henry Leland's masterpiece would become but another minor footnote in the cluttered fine print of automotive history.

As early as July, 1921, the Lelands, Henry and Wilfred, had approached Henry Ford for a loan, then eventually suggested a friendly takeover. After consultations with his son, Henry Ford decided to purchase Lincoln at a receiver's sale set for February 4, 1922. The price: 8 million dollars. On the day of the purchase he stated to reporters: "We have built more cars than anyone else, and now we are going to build a better car than anyone else."

One of the greatest group portraits in automotive history was taken on the occasion. In the Lincoln administrative offices, under the watchful gaze of the Great Emancipator himself (peering down on the proceedings from no less than four portraits of various sizes and descriptions), the papers were signed. The founders of the two firms, the two Henrys, stand impassively at the back, while their sons are seated at an ornate table. It is the faces of Wilfred Leland and Edsel Ford that draw one's attention. Wilfred, the older of the two, is downcast, somber. Edsel, in contrast, is full of energy, his feet resting informally against the table legs, while he stares with youthful authority at the camera lens—the only one of the four to do so. It has to be one of the most compelling depictions of a "changing of the guard" encounter ever recorded.

Henry Ford received a tremendous amount of favorable free publicity for what was perceived as his good Samaritan deed. It was not, however, a marriage made in heaven. The Lelands were under the impression that they were going to continue to run Lincoln with almost complete autonomy under Ford ownership. Edsel could have told them that wasn't going to happen.

Frictions were inevitable, and by June 13th the Lelands were gone for good. Henry and Wilfred Leland, who had been president and vice-president, respectively, were replaced by Edsel (formerly second vice-president) and Ernest C. Kanzler, Edsel's brother-in-law.

Edsel Ford's 1923 Lincoln Coupe.

The Lelands ultimately sued the Fords, claiming that they were promised autonomy to operate the company under Ford ownership and also that Ford Motor Company would compensate Lincoln stockholders. The Fords categorically denied that any such promises were made. Although a voluntary payment of $4,018,699 was made to over 900 creditors (and seven company directors who had signed notes) in March, 1923, no compensation was ever forthcoming for the benefit of Lincoln stockholders. The battle continued all the way to the Michigan Supreme Court, but the final ruling, handed down in 1931, was in the Fords' favor. The Lelands then threw in the towel. Henry Leland died the following year.[3]

There is one fact about which even the Lelands must have agreed with the Fords, however: after their departure, Lincoln quality remained high. In fact, if styling is taken into account, the [Edsel] Ford-built Lincolns were soon superior.

Edsel Ford was just the man Lincoln needed. The Lelands had provided the best chassis that they knew how to build, and now Edsel was determined to clothe it with coachwork of equal quality. It was a task he approached with relish. His method was to solicit designs from the leading coachbuilders of the day—LeBaron, Locke, Judkins, Fleetwood (before it was swallowed up by General Motors), Brunn, Dietrich, Murray, and so on—and then order

Henry and Edsel with the Prince of Wales touring the Lincoln Factory in 1924.

Edsel and Eleanor Ford Estate on Lake St. Clair.

selected designs in lots of 50 or 100 or more. In this fashion, Edsel was able to offer the highest quality designs at prices far below what would have been charged for one-offs. Everyone profited from this system, especially Edsel, who at last had one area of undiluted personal responsibility.

Running Lincoln seemed to be the boost he needed. The 1920s were a decade of remarkable and varied activity for the younger Ford. In the first place, he and Eleanor were industriously building a family. Henry II had been born in 1917, followed by Benson in 1919, Josephine in 1923, and William Clay in 1925. In 1926–27, the two of them built a splendid home on the shores of Lake St. Clair on land bought by Henry Ford in 1911–13.

The sixty-room mansion, which sat on an eighty-seven-acre estate with over half-a-mile of lake frontage, was designed by noted architect, Albert Kahn, who used as his inspiration the Cotswold area of England. Noted landscape architect Jens Jensen did the grounds. A beautifully crafted sandstone building, the house resembled an English country manor. Among the amenities was a power plant that provided a private supply of power to the estate, a trick Edsel picked up from his father at Fairlane. A large reception hall handled the three public rooms on the main floor; all functioned as drawing rooms. Also on the main floor was the large dining room with no electrical outlets; the Fords preferred to dine by candlelight. The house had a working fireplace in every room.

From Edsel's perspective, the best thing about living on his estate may have been that it was clear across town from Dearborn and his father. Henry Ford's open contempt for Edsel's Grosse Pointe society friends was well known. It was rumored that he had his son under surveillance and even bribed several household staff members for any kind of information.

Regardless, Edsel became an active participant in civic affairs and patron of the arts. In contrast to his father, who didn't believe in charity, he became one of the largest annual donors to Detroit area charities.[4] He also served for many years as president of the Detroit Arts Commission and hired Diego Rivera to do the celebrated murals that adorn the walls at the Detroit Institute of Arts.

In addition, Edsel was instrumental in arranging the financing for Admiral Richard E. Byrd's historic flight over the North Pole in 1926. At the beginning of his polar expedition, Byrd paused to pay special thanks to the man who had made it possible:

> The expedition would have been impossible without the help and encouragement I received from Edsel Ford, who has a deep and sincere interest in the development of aviation. Mr. Ford's unselfish interest and sportsmanship impressed me when without the slightest hesitation he gave me permission to purchase for the expedition a plane that will be in competition with a three-motor plane that he is developing.[5]

The Edsel Ford family and Clara Ford, about 1927. *Left to right*, William Clay, Eleanor, Benson, Clara, Edsel, Josephine, and Henry II.

Byrd was referring to the soon-to-be-famous Ford Trimotor. The polar expedition flew a Dutch-built Fokker, but, perhaps in compensation, Byrd named it the "Josephine Ford," after Edsel's daughter. When, following the expedition, debts still plagued Byrd, Edsel Ford bought the Fokker, and it resides today in the Henry Ford Museum.

The next time Byrd tackled the polar reaches, he did so in a Ford Trimotor. In November, 1929, Byrd launched an expedition to overfly the South Pole and accomplished the feat on November 29th. Again, Edsel Ford led the effort to finance the expedition, giving $90,000 in equipment and materials and arranging financial contributions. In gratitude, Byrd named several geographic sites in the Antarctic for Edsel, including the Edsel Ford Range of mountains in Marie Byrd Land, Ford Island, Ford Massif, Ford Nunataks, and Ford Peak. Edsel's daughter was honored again, as well, with Mount Josephine in the Alexandria Mountains.

Meanwhile, back at the ranch, Edsel had finally convinced his father to put the Model T out to pasture. It had not been easy. The blood-letting within the company over that decision reached the highest executive levels when Ernest Kanzler was fired. His fate spoke volumes about life at Ford Motor Company in the 1920s.

Kanzler had been in charge of production at the Highland Park plant, then had helped develop Ford's expansive chain of assembly facilities around the world. In addition, he served in an important role in marketing operations. In 1924, he had been elected second vice-president of the Ford Motor Company. His ace in the hole was his relationship to Edsel. It was also his undoing, for it caused the elder Ford to become jealous of him. It was Kanzler's opposition to the Model T, however, that directly triggered his downfall.

In 1926, Kanzler wrote a memo saying, in effect, that the Model T was dated, the competition was running rings around it, and, for the sake of the company, it had to go. For his trouble, Henry Ford saw to it that Kanzler was subsequently ignored, snubbed, slighted, and, in general, humiliated at every opportunity and in every imaginable way. Then, when Edsel was out of the country and unable even to protest, Kanzler was summarily terminated. His treatment was vintage Henry Ford at the Old Man's worst.

Unfortunately, Henry Ford's worst was increasingly becoming the norm. Success beyond mortal dreams had not softened him. If anything it convinced him of his own brilliance and omnipotence, and prompted him to become ever more isolated and set in his ways. This process had a corrosive effect on Ford Motor Company, turning it gradually into a virtual dictatorship, and left it ill-suited to confront the challenges posed by enlightened competitors, such

Henry and Edsel standing with a Ford Model A.

as Alfred Sloan at General Motors. In an "autobiography" published under his
name in the early 1920s—but almost certainly written by one of his public relations retainers—Ford outlined in no uncertain terms his ideas regarding the
cold-blooded role of industrial management:

> It is not necessary to have meetings to establish good feelings between indi-
> viduals or departments. There is not much personal contact [at Ford Motor
> Company]—the men do their work and go home. A factory is not a drawing
> room. We do not believe in the "glad hand," or the professionalized "personal
> touch," or "human element." I pity the poor fellow who is so soft and flabby
> that he must always have an atmosphere of good feeling around him before he
> can do his work.[6]

How Edsel must have cringed as he read those words.

At any rate, after years of foot-dragging, and as if calculated to make matters worse, the decision to drop the Model T finally came with such sudden-
ness that there was no replacement even on the drawing boards. This had the
practical effect of leaving Ford dealers with nothing to sell for months and
giving Chevrolet a golden opportunity upon which it brilliantly capitalized to
Ford's lasting detriment. The new car—called the Model "A" when it came—
was (almost) worth the wait. Most impressive of all was the scaled-down Lincoln styling, done under the careful direction of Edsel. Model A sales took off,
and even Henry had to admit his son knew how a car should look.

Edsel likewise took an active interest in Ford's export markets. In 1929, he turned the first spade full of dirt at the Dagenham factory in England destined to become one of the most important Ford production sites outside America. Ernest Kanzler had personally selected the site six year earlier.

Also by this time, Edsel had Lincoln running so smoothly it reported a profit of $2 million in 1929. The Leland-designed L-Series Lincolns were moving toward the end of their life cycle, though, and a replacement would soon be needed.

Why Edsel moved backward in the alphabet in search of a designation for his new model is unknown. Perhaps this first Ford-designed Lincoln series was supposed to recall the last luxury car built by Ford—the Ford Model K of

Posed at the 1932 Indianapolis 500. *Left to right*, Eddie Rickenbacker, Henry, Edsel (seated at the wheel of a Lincoln KB-Series), Harvey Firestone, Jr., Henry II, Benson, and Harvey Firestone, Sr.

1931 Lincoln K.

1906. In any case, the 1931 Lincoln K-Series was, by all accounts, a splendid machine and a worthy successor to the Leland-designed L-Series.

In the turbulent years of the 1930s, the mighty K-Series Lincoln gave as good a fight as any luxury marque, and a better one than most, but nothing seemed to work in a market that was vanishing day-by-day. As Edsel would later remark, "We did not stop producing luxury cars; people stopped buying them."[7]

As early as 1932, Lincoln was in deep trouble. Fortunately, help was on the way.

CHAPTER TWO

The Edsel Ford Family, circa 1937. *Left to right*, Edsel, Eleanor,
Henry II, Benson, Josephine, and William Clay.

Edsel Ford: The Final Years

THE LINCOLN-ZEPHYR was conceived in 1932, a product of the profound concerns of W. O. Briggs and Edsel Ford. Briggs, head of the Briggs Body Company, had long been a prime supplier of bodies to Ford. Lately, though, Ford felt that Briggs was paying too much attention to its rapidly expanding Chrysler business. To counter this feeling, Howard Bonbright, a personal friend of Edsel, was hired to manage financial policy and, specifically, to improve relations with Ford Motor Company. In addition, John Tjaarda was directed to develop a new car that might be salable to Ford management.

John Tjaarda van Sterkenburg was an enormously talented Dutch automotive designer who had come to the United States in 1923. He first landed a job with Locke, the custom body builders, and later worked for General Motors' pioneering styling department under the celebrated Harley Earl. While with General Motors, he began working on a radical series of streamlined dream cars, most of which were rear-engined, or mid-engined unibody designs. When W. O. Briggs told him to work up a totally new car for possible Ford manufacture, he naturally drew heavily on these studies. Proceeding under tight security, he soon had preliminary sketches and a structural model ready for presentation. At this juncture, a meeting was arranged with Edsel.

Edsel, too, was a worried man in 1932. Lincoln operations had been the one area where he had been allowed a relatively free hand, but with Lincoln awash in red ink, even that lone sanctuary was threatened. When Briggs unveiled Tjaarda's proposal for a new car, Edsel saw it as a godsend: a car that could be developed into a medium-priced Lincoln. Best of all, it could be developed on the sly at Briggs where Henry Ford and his ever-spying cronies would be unable to interfere.

Accordingly, Tjaarda continued to work away almost alone in his fifth floor office. (Briggs was also heavily involved in the Chrysler Airflow project at this time, so that was one more reason for top security.) Several mornings a week, Edsel would stop in on his way to work to check on the progress. He and Tjaarda soon developed a cordial relationship. Tjaarda was later to write that "it was truly a pleasure to be associated with an individual of such good taste and discernment as Edsel Ford."[1]

With Tjaarda working on the body structure, Frank Johnson, Lincoln's chief engineer, set to work on the drivetrain, principally the Zephyr V12 powerplant. The V12 was basically a scaled-up Ford V8 and the rest of the Zephyr chassis was also scaled-up Ford, complete with old-fashioned Ford mechanical brakes, a solid front axle, and transverse leaf springs.

The Zephyr was designed throughout under Edsel's supervision, though this proved a mixed blessing in certain respects. It did not receive the degree of engineering development a Ford car would have had and the chassis—especially the engine—suffered for it. The V12 has long been recognized as the weak point of the design and bears the greatest responsibility for the Zephyr's checkered reputation. Many of the V12's problems were attended to during the ten model years of production, but some were never adequately addressed and, in sum, the engine was not well regarded in or out of the company.

Still, the Zephyr as originally conceived was a visual hit at the 1936 auto shows, overshadowed only slightly by the stunning Cord 810. The Zephyr was not the first mass production streamlined car—the Chrysler and De Soto Airflows and the Hupp Aerodynamic had been introduced in 1934—but it was the first one that met with broad public acceptance.

In most respects, the Zephyr was outstanding. Edsel had seen to it that the fit and finish were of a high order. Even the chassis met with a surprising amount of praise at the time, despite the fact that the braking and suspension systems were already quite dated in 1936. Most importantly, the Zephyr sold very well against its prime competition, the Packard 120 and the Cadillac La Salle. In short, the Lincoln-Zephyr had achieved all of the goals set for it by W. O. Briggs and Edsel Ford.

1936 Lincoln-Zephyr.

By 1936 or 1937, though, it was obvious to Edsel and Ford's highly regarded national sales chief, Jack Davis, that Ford Motor Company desperately needed yet another medium-priced entry to fill the gap that existed in the high-volume end of the medium-price field between the Ford and the new Lincoln-Zephyr. As the economy began to rebound from the depths of the depression, this was where the shrewd money knew the sales growth would be greatest. As it stood, Ford sales people felt as if they were simply grooming customers for General Motors, Chrysler, and the mid-priced independents. In particular, General Motors, under the decentralized management structure and shrewd, blanket-the-market strategy of Alfred Sloan, was brilliantly exploiting all of Ford Motor Company's weaknesses. Worse, Chrysler Corporation was following the same basic plan with equally good results. In fact, in 1936 Chrysler had surged past Ford to become the nation's second largest automaker. It wasn't hard to figure out why.

Building a good car was not enough; it was necessary to sell it to someone, and there were four basic target groups: 1) existing customers; 2) customers graduating up from less-expensive brands sold by the same company; 3) customers graduating up from less-expensive brands sold by other companies; and 4) customers "captured" from other brands in the same price segments. Indeed, these categories are still valid today.

Of the four categories, the first is the Mother Lode. An old axiom in the marketing profession is that "a customer is yours to lose," i.e., once someone is buying your product or service, he or she is going to tend to continue to do so until given a compelling reason to change buying habits. Unfortunately, owing to Henry Ford's obsession with the Model T, a large percentage of Ford's customer base had been squandered in the 1920s.

The second category—customers graduating up from less-expensive brands sold by the same company—was also a killer from Ford Motor Company's perspective. Except for the Lincoln-Zephyr, which was a marginal competitor at the upper fringe of the medium-priced field, Ford Motor Company had no medium-priced entries at all. In stark contrast, General Motors offered a full range of cars spanning the price spectrum so that customers could move up or down the scale, as desire or financial circumstance dictated, while still remaining in the General Motors fold. When they outgrew Chevrolet, they could walk down the street to the Olds or Buick dealer. Ford cultivated thousands of customers for GM's and Chrysler's mid-priced cars in the 1930s and 1940s.

The third category—customers graduating up from less expensive brands sold by other companies—was another one in which Ford Motor Company was a loser, and for the same reasons it was out of contention in the second category.

The fourth category—customers "captured" from other brands in the same price classes—was also one in which Ford Motor Company suffered grievously. Even in greatly improved form, thanks to Edsel's insistence on contemporary styling, the 1936 Ford was unable to attract many buyers who weren't already in the Ford fold. It was increasingly obsolete mechanically, and Henry Ford resolutely resisted most of Edsel's attempts to remedy shortcomings that were obvious to everyone but the Old Man. As for the medium-priced market, that was a near total bust. Ford Motor Company had no volume product line (other than the Zephyr) with which to even mount an effort, and there was considerable doubt that Henry Ford would allow one to be built.

Edsel decided to try. He understood the need and knew that unless he acted on his own to do something about it no one would. So, as with the Lincoln-Zephyr, the Mercury was Edsel's project all the way. The effort probably began in the early part of 1937, although there is no conclusive evidence. Larry Sheldrick, Ford's de facto chief engineer, later recalled that it was first discussed with him in July, 1937, but it was more than likely well along before he heard about it.

Unlike the Zephyr project, though, which had been farmed out to Briggs, the Mercury would be done in-house. Edsel had established a styling department in 1935 under the direction of Eugene Turrenne "Bob" Gregorie. By 1937, Gregorie had built a nineteen-man styling staff, including seven apprentices.

Of course, there was other work to be done. Those nineteen men were entrusted with responsibility for designing not only the new Mercury, but the 1939–40 Ford lines, face-lifting the Lincoln-Zephyr for 1939 and creating an entirely new one for 1940, creating the first one-off Continental, and the full range of Ford commercial vehicles, to boot. That they achieved as much as they did is certainly testimony to their ability and hard work. It also says a lot about Edsel, how much he cared about design and, not least, the degree to which he had managed to assume personal control over that end of the business.

The styling department was located in the engineering building, but Bob Gregorie flatly refused to take orders from Sheldrick, sparking a running conflict between the two. Willys P. Wagner, one of Gregorie's stylists, recalled:

> [Bob] refused to knuckle under to Sheldrick. . . . He worked only for Edsel
> Ford, nobody else. . . . Back in those days, almost anything could happen.
> The boys up at the top, they were all jockeying for positions. Anybody who
> thought he could fire somebody and get away with it did it.[2]

In the factionalized company at that time, Sheldrick was allied with the elder Ford, while the styling staff worked for Edsel. Ross Cousins, a new arrival in 1938, recalled:

Henry Bennett.

We just had this one corner of the engineering lab. Henry didn't like us too well, but Edsel was our godfather and patron saint. . . .

There was so much political crap going on that they used to drill holes in the partition to spy on [Gregorie]. They had the watchman at the gate checking him in, checking him out, just so they might be able to get something on him so they could fire him, but they didn't. It was people like [Harry] Bennett [Ford's personnel director] and the top engineer, Sheldrick. They'd even come into our department and look in the toilet, look under the doors to see if we were in there too long. We had to almost fight for our existence.[3]

This situation is all the more appalling when one considers that styling was clearly Edsel's domain—the domain of the nominal president of Ford Motor Company—and it was his staff, in effect, that was under constant siege by people close to his own father. Bennett's rise to prominence in the company in the 1930s was a particularly bitter pill. More than once Edsel contemplated his resignation as Bennett's hold over his father became stronger. Bennett, a former prize-fighter, had been brought in by Henry Ford to secure labor peace and soon, according to most accounts, became like a son to the elder Ford— or a Svengali, depending on the version of the story being related. What seems clear is that Edsel's relationship with his father deteriorated as his father's dependence on the thuggish Bennett increased. Charlie Sorensen, in his memoirs, succinctly described Bennett and also had a few words to say about Bennett's staff:

He was a flamboyant character who delighted in being spectacularly mysterious and his cops-and-robbers activities fascinated the older Ford. . . .

He had a strange collection of broken bruisers, ex-baseball players, one-time football stars and recently-freed jailbirds. They never looked or acted like Ford men and Edsel and I were continually apologizing for their bad manners.[4]

By this point, all the really progressive people in the Ford organization had naturally gravitated toward Edsel, which nearly always ended up putting them at risk when Henry grew jealous of their friendship with his son. Ernest Kanzler, Edsel's brother-in-law, was an early victim of this dynamic. Jack Davis, Ford's sales manager, suffered a similar fate shortly after the Mercury was introduced. Both returned to help Henry Ford II resurrect the company after the war. Of Edsel's immediate circle, only John Crawford, his executive assistant, and Bob Gregorie managed to hang onto their posts until his death. Recalled Crawford in later years:

Bob Gregorie was the originator, a young man with ideas whom Edsel took under his wing and handled with kid gloves. I was the modifier. I had to figure out how or if the car could be built. Could we form a sheet of steel to the desired shape? Was chrome trim practical? And so on. But, Edsel was the inspirer. Without him, none of those beautiful cars would have even existed.[5]

Gregorie shed further light on the special working relationship:

Mr. [Edsel] Ford had an instinctive liking for dignity in an automobile, but dignity that reflected its purpose. A dignified car could still look fast and active—sporting, exhilarating. The only people making such cars in our day were the small companies and the custom body builders, and they were all going out of business. . . . He always had the dream of combining the beauty of custom design with the low cost of production in quantity. In spite of serious difficulties—some personal but mainly the tradition that said it couldn't be done—he kept planting the seed and encouraging it to sprout.

Mr. Ford had me set up the first true styling section the company ever had with three or four men at the start. He set up no rules. I had every chance to express myself. I didn't even keep regular hours. Sometimes I'd just take off for a long trip in a car to clear my brain. Mr. Ford respected imagination and talent—and such respect was rare, I can tell you, in the old automobile companies. . . . Edsel Ford alone seemed to appreciate that this industry is a combination of vision, production, and sales. He had the vision. I did the work of translating his vision into workable designs.[6]

Twenty years later, when the ill-fated Edsel car was built, Ford publicists recalled this story:

In the styling department, Gregorie kept a number of old prototype cars for reference. They stood in a dark corner covered with dust sheets. At moments when business affairs grew too oppressive, Edsel Ford would appear in the studio, climb into one of the sheeted cars, and beckon to his lieutenant. "There he would sit," Gregorie recalls, "in the cool dark, to meditate and to talk. Mr. Ford seemed to just relax. He would talk of anything that came into his head, such as boats, in which we had a common interest."[7]

From an engineering standpoint, the Mercury drew heavily on Ford technology as had the Lincoln-Zephyr before it. Actually, the 239 cubic inch Mercury engine was created for Ford police application. It was essentially the same as the 221 cubic inch Ford V8 with a 1/8-inch larger bore created by deletion of a 1/8-inch sleeve. The rest of the chassis was likewise similar, although the body was more-or-less unique to the Mercury in 1939 and 1940.[8] After that, it fell into the Ford body cycle.

In practice, the vast similarities between the Ford and the Mercury worked to the detriment of the latter. And, while the body was essentially different, there was little obvious effort toward establishing a unique Mercury identity with it. To the contrary, this was family resemblance with a vengeance and indicated a real perceptional failing on Edsel's part. He even wanted to sell the car under the "Ford-Mercury" nameplate, much as the Zephyr had been a hyphenated Lincoln. What he seemed not to understand was that it was far easier to sell a discounted Lincoln than an inflated Ford. In fact, this sparked one of the few real arguments between Gregorie and his patron. Gregorie recalled:

> One of the most interesting things about the 1939 Mercury—the development of it—was the difficulty Mr. Edsel Ford seemed to have in grasping the idea of what this car was going to be. Oddly enough, he wasn't trying to step up far enough from the basic Ford. His whole concept was to tie it in with the Ford, and it was very difficult for me to get the point across. He was very touchy on the subject. In other words, to make this an effective car, we thought that every effort should be made to dissuade the public that the Mercury was just a blown-up Ford, which, of course, it really was. . . .
>
> Mr. Ford even insisted on the hubcaps being embossed with "Ford-Mercury." He became very incensed when I tried to dissuade him from doing that and, as a matter of fact, he blew up one afternoon. He said, "What's wrong with the name Ford? It's been good for forty years, hasn't it?" When the car was presented at the New York show, why the sales people all came after me and said, "My gosh, we've got to get the name Ford off this car!"[9]

On the other hand, there are those who believe that Edsel's determination to call it a Ford reflected his fear of upsetting his father and the palace guard, who perhaps didn't want a new car line at all. In any case, Edsel reluctantly agreed with Gregorie and the sales people, and the name had been changed by the official press introduction on October 24, 1938. Most of the early promotional materials, however, carried the rejected Ford-Mercury logo, since it was too late to alter them all before the official public introduction on November 4th.

The new Mercury was one of the highlights at the Ford pavilion at the 1939 New York World's Fair. The pavilion was another one of Edsel's projects. In fact, Edsel loved the fair so much he rented a house nearby and spent weeks in attendance, much of it mixing with visitors, official and otherwise, to the Ford exhibit.

George Pierrot, a Ford publicist who worked at the Ford pavilion, recalled that, due to Edsel's instructions, it had an exceptionally well-stocked wine cellar. Edsel was determined that Ford's guests—including top-ranking government leaders from at home and abroad—should be treated to the best hospitality the company could offer. When Henry Ford visited the exhibit, however, the wine cellar was locked up and everyone—apparently including the elder Ford himself—pretended it did not exist.

If the new Mercury lacked something in styling identity, Edsel more than

1939 Mercury.

made up for it with his next project: the first Lincoln Continental. The original idea was to create a custom one-off for his personal use with no stated plans to put it into volume production. As fate would have it, it was destined to be his last such car—and his finest.

In fact, a major—if unspoken—reason for the Continental may have been the impending death of the K-Series Lincoln. Edsel's ambitious proposal for a successor to the mighty K had been rejected and the Lincoln brand was in desperate need of a prestige line at the top. The Continental saved the day, and, given the Byzantine inner workings of the Ford empire at this juncture, it is at least plausible that its inspiration was not entirely innocent.

Whatever the motivations, the project began in September, 1938, when Edsel returned from Europe with ideas for a convertible coupe to be built with distinctively European lines. Moreover, it had to be built in time for his Florida vacation that winter. Edsel's first thought was to use the Ford chassis, or possibly that of the soon-to-be-announced Mercury. It was Gregorie who suggested the Lincoln-Zephyr.

That decided, a crayon sketch was made on a 1/10 scale Zephyr blueprint, and from that a 1/10 clay model was fashioned. The details were all executed

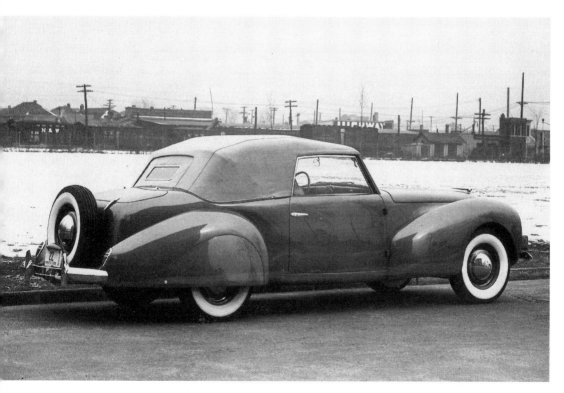

1939 Lincoln Continental prototype.

to Edsel's specifications using of as many off-the-shelf Zephyr parts as practical, although many were sectioned, and cut-down or lengthened. The only truly unique aspect of the car was the rear with its exposed spare tire.

In October, 1938, Edsel approved the clay model and directed that a full-size body draft—or drawing—be made, thus bypassing the usual full-sized clay model. Martin Regitko did the draft, and then Henry Cornelius, who was in charge of Lincoln body engineering, set to work producing the actual body panels. The panels were hand-hammered over wooden forms and put together with enormous quantities of solder. The finished car weighed over 5,000 pounds. It was completed in the latter part of February, 1939, and shipped to Florida, where Edsel was vacationing at his Hobe Sound estate.

Edsel was enthusiastic. More to the point, his friends in Hobe Sound and Palm Beach—a circle which included much of the cream of the social register—were enthusiastic, too, and, according to the oft-told story (which may even be true), placed orders for upwards of two hundred copies should he decide to put the Continental into production. This, he did.

However it came to pass, the Lincoln-Zephyr Continental was officially announced to the public on October 2, 1939, with only comparatively minor changes required to make it suitable for volume manufacture. The rest, as they say, is history. The Continental remained in production until 1948. It was beloved from the start and became an instant classic as soon as the last one rolled from the factory.

The remainder of the Zephyr line was also fresh for 1940, having been given its first all-new sheet metal since its inception. Despite this, the new models were not notably successful in the marketplace. This sluggishness was probably not so much a reflection on the cars as it was on Henry Ford himself who had, over the years, systematically alienated vast segments of the market with ill-advised battles against the Jews, the Federal Government, big business, the labor movement, and on and on ad nauseam. Just about the only group to escape Henry's wrath were white, Anglo-Saxon, Protestant farmers. (One wag noted that Henry Ford had single-handedly managed to give bigotry a bad name.) By 1940, Ford's conflict with the United Auto Workers (UAW) was reaching its bloody climax and many Ford, Mercury, and Lincoln prospects were turned off by the spectacle. The antiquated mechanicals of Ford vehicles didn't help much, either, nor did the increasingly unfavorable reputation of the Zephyr's V12 engine. In sum, it was not the best time to be selling Ford products, but it was indicative of the rapidly deteriorating situation within Ford Motor Company itself.

Edsel had a few other notable victories during the later years of his life. He finally convinced his father to allow the company's products to be fitted with hydraulic brakes beginning with the 1939 model run. The Ford six-cylinder engine was a much harder sell.

Henry Ford hated the very thought of a six. Chevrolet had one-upped him in 1929 with its first six, the so-called "stovebolt" engine. Chevrolet, in turn, was scooped when Ford switched to its new V8 in 1932. Unfortunately, many buyers wanted the economy of a six and Ford sales suffered as a consequence throughout the 1930s. For years, no one could prevail upon the Old Man to build a six. Finally, though, Edsel and others deeply concerned with Ford's deteriorating sales position secured permission to build the Ford six that first ap-

Edsel and Benson Ford yachting on Lake Saint Claire.

peared during the 1941 model year. Independent front suspension was a lost cause, though.[10] It was not until after Henry's death that Ford products got modern chassis components.

Normal development work on Ford, Mercury, and Lincoln lines was proceeding when the United States entered the war in December, 1941. New Fords and Mercurys were being developed for the 1943 model year as per their usual two-year cycle. The Zephyr, with its unibody construction and lower production volume, was on a much longer cycle, with another new body on line for 1944, or thereabouts. Well-developed clays existed as early as September, 1941, and represented the last major styling project overseen by Edsel. They give testimony to the love affair he and Bob Gregorie were having with fastback styling.

Of course, wartime work completely monopolized the energies of the company after Pearl Harbor. Larry Sheldrick told of an episode relating to the testing of one of the original Jeep prototypes. He had managed, without telling Edsel, to slip Henry II and Benson into the test vehicle, then had them pull right up to their surprised and elated father. Recalled Sheldrick:

> That was the one time that I saw Edsel when he was thoroughly enjoying himself. He was awfully proud of his boys.[11]

The internal situation in Ford Motor Company was becoming even more turbulent as the decade drew on. By 1942, both Henry and Edsel were ailing, the elder Ford suffering from old age and periods of senility, the younger Ford suffering the ravages of stomach ulcers brought on by stress. In early 1942, he was operated on for these ulcers and placed on a strict diet during his convalescence.

A bitter and debilitating power struggle enveloped the company. It had been brewing for years between the group loyal to Henry and Bennett, on the one hand, and that loyal to Edsel and Sorensen on the other. As the two Fords waned in strength, the battle gained added urgency. One by one, middle and upper level executives either quit or were unceremoniously fired, thus progressively gutting the company of its most talented people.

Irving Bacon had been the company's official artist-in-residence for many years, but never brought his lunch to work. He once explained this to a new employee by saying, "I've only been there thirty-some years, and I'm not sure I'll be there at lunch time to eat it."

Another vignette from the "Mad Hatter Era" at Ford Motor Company (as some Ford historians have characterized it) comes from John Conde, a former public relations executive at American Motors. Conde was hired by Fred Black at Nash-Kelvinator in 1945. Black, in turn, had served as one of Henry Ford's close associates for nearly a quarter of a century until he was fired in 1942. According to Conde, Black would never drop a memo or letter into a wastepaper basket without tearing it into many pieces. Recalled Conde:

> I asked him one day why he did that.
>
> "Oh," Black answered, "that was something Mr. Ford always said we should do. We always tore up everything, and sometimes we were ordered to deposit some of the torn pieces in one basket and some in another, so no one could ever find out what we were doing."[12]

In early 1943, Edsel went under the knife again because of problems related to his ulcers. This time the doctors found inoperable stomach cancer. He also suffered from undulant fever, and it has long been assumed that he contracted this fever from drinking unpasteurized milk from his father's farm as part of his ulcer diet. On May 26, 1943, he died. He was forty-nine.

Many who knew and loved Edsel blamed Henry for his untimely death. Edsel's mother, Clara, reportedly did not speak to her husband for weeks thereafter, and Eleanor, Edsel's wife, never forgave the Old Man. For his part, Henry was devastated by his son's death. Bennett recalled the following exchange:

> After Edsel's death Mr. Ford was disturbed about the relationship he had had with his son. He couldn't keep away from the subject. . . .
>
> "Harry," he once said to me, "do you honestly think I was ever cruel to Edsel?"
>
> It wasn't easy to answer that one directly, and I temporized: "Well, if that had been me you'd treated that way, it wouldn't have been cruelty."
>
> But Mr. Ford wasn't satisfied. "Why don't you give me an honest answer?"
>
> So I said, "Well, cruel no; but unfair, yes." And then I added, "If that had been me, I'd have got mad."
>
> Mr. Ford seized on that: "That's what I wanted him to do—get mad."[13]

In the aftermath of Edsel's death, the twenty-three-year-old Henry Ford II was quickly discharged from the Navy and brought into the company as a vice-president. Ernest Kanzler returned to act as family advisor to the young man. Sorensen, who was by then in his sixties and sick of the daily turmoil, stuck around long enough to make sure Henry II was established as heir apparent. Old Henry, however, insisted upon reassuming the presidency, a position held by his late son since 1919. This action was almost certainly prompted by Bennett, who hoped to legitimize his own bold grab for power by exerting control over the Old Man.

John Bugas was with the FBI in Detroit and had investigated Bennett on

Left to right, Charles Sorensen, Henry I, and Henry II posed together in December, 1943.

more than one occasion, reportedly at the behest of Edsel. Bennett subsequently hired him only to have him transfer his loyalty to Edsel's young son in the ensuing power struggle.

Bugas, a top executive in the postwar Ford era from 1944 to 1968, recalled that Bennett boasted that he had a salary of "only" $40,000 or so with the Ford Motor Company in the 1940s (still not a shabby amount of money back then).[14] But, added Bugas, Bennett had access to the company's funds and had several homes built with Ford-bought materials and labor. After Edsel's death, Bennett would issue orders in the elder Ford's name and no one knew whether they came from Ford or from Bennett—and no one had the courage to ask. Bennett, according to Bugas, had the mind of a thug and always conducted business in an under-the-table fashion because that was the only way he knew.

The crisis finally came to a head in late September, 1945, when a united Ford family at last prevailed upon Henry to abdicate in favor of his grandson.

The Ford family circa 1975.

Reportedly, Eleanor threatened to sell her Ford Motor Company stock if Henry refused—a not inconsiderable threat considering that the company was privately held until 1956.

Eleanor Clay Ford died on October 19, 1976, at the age of 80. She left an estate estimated at close to $90,000,000. She had, throughout the remainder of her life, continued Edsel's work as a patron of the arts in Detroit and as a noted civic leader. After her passing, she was temporarily laid to rest in the Hudson mausoleum at Detroit's Woodlawn Cemetery until the tomb in which her husband had long been interred could be opened.

The Edsel Ford tomb, built of black granite, is surrounded by a remarkable selection of the movers and shakers in the early auto industry: John and Horace Dodge; James Couzens; C. Harold Wills; Roy D. Chapin, Sr.; George Holley; Robert C. Hupp; K. T. Keller; Bill Metzger; and Harry Jewett; among others. It is fittingly elevated company for a man of Edsel's achievements. Indeed, though Edsel was little appreciated in his lifetime, he may have achieved far more than any of them.

It was Edsel who persuaded his father to buy the Lincoln Motor Company at a receiver's sale in 1922. It was Edsel who finally persuaded his father to retire the antiquated Model T. It was Edsel who then directed the highly successful styling of the Model A, which, as much as anything else, put that all-important model across with the public. It was Edsel who saved Lincoln in the depths of the depression by creating the upper medium-priced Lincoln-Zephyr. It was Edsel who saw the need for a mainstream medium-priced car to enable Ford Motor Company to compete head-to-head with General Motors and Chrysler, and created the Mercury. And, not least, it was Edsel who gave the company the three sons who would, after their father's death, save it from their senile grandfather and his thuggish cronies.

It is not to belittle Henry Ford II's immense achievements in the postwar era to say that it is hard to imagine what the company would look like today divorced from the benefit of his father's contributions. Indeed, one wonders: Without Edsel Ford's contributions, would there even be a Ford Motor Company today? He had succeeded in putting in place most of the essential pieces that would be needed to make the postwar recovery possible. Had he outlived his father, there is every reason to believe that he would have achieved as much as his son.

Yet, of all the indignities Edsel endured, one of the cruelest must surely have been one that transpired after his death: the naming of the Edsel automobile. Thus, even though it came about more than a decade after his demise, the best-known fiasco—at least to the general public—in the automobile industry history remains indelibly associated with Edsel Ford.

CHAPTER THREE

1926 Pontiac.

Development of the Market

TO UNDERSTAND THE EDSEL—why it had to be created, why it was what it was, and why it failed—it is absolutely essential to understand the development of the Ford Motor Company, and particularly the massive failure of that company to comprehend and respond to the development of the medium-priced field. It is also vital to understand the intense competitive pressures exerted upon Ford Motor Company by the achievements of Henry Ford's principal competitor, Alfred Sloan at General Motors. If Henry Ford was the manufacturing genius in the development of the modern automobile industry, Sloan was the one who developed the modern management system to go with it. Sloan also recognized the fundamental changes in the market after World War I and devised, to Ford's lasting detriment, a brilliant marketing strategy to exploit them.

The highly segmented market we know today was not always there. In fact, in the earliest days of the industry, there were no recognizable market segments at all. There were just "good" cars and "bad" cars, although it was not always easy to tell which was which.

As the automobile began to be taken seriously as a means of transportation, however, two basic market segments quickly developed. The low-priced cars that were designed to sell to the ordinary citizen constituted one segment. This was the segment that Henry Ford strove to serve and, with his fabulously successful Model T, finally did. Still, the Model T, for all its utility and affordability, was a fairly dreadful machine. Wags quickly claimed that the name "Ford" stood for "Fix Or Repair Daily," but people kept buying them because they were cheap and, if they required constant maintenance, they were at least easy and inexpensive to fix.

On the other end of the spectrum was the quality car. These were cars designed for maximum performance, reliability, and durability as those terms were understood at the time. A number of important competitors soon came into being. By 1910, Americans were already speaking of the "Three P's of Motoring"—Packard, Peerless, and Pierce-Arrow. Together with Cadillac and Winton, these were probably considered the top five leaders in the quality field, although additional brands were important as well, including Apperson, Chalmers, Franklin, Locomobile, Marmon, Stearns, Stevens-Duryea, and a few others.

The word "quality" as a descriptive of this second segment is used intentionally. This was the segment of the market we would speak of as the "luxury" segment today, although the entire market was still in embryonic form at this point. It is difficult to speak in terms of a "luxury" car market in the sense that such a market came into existence around the time of World War I. For one thing, the cars in it varied widely in price. For another, they weren't necessarily luxurious. In fact, Henry Leland, the remarkable man who played a key role in developing both Cadillac (in 1903) and Lincoln (in 1920), would no doubt have bridled at the term. Leland's mindset in this regard can be gauged from his description of the first L-Series Lincolns. He described them as:

> substantial, well-proportioned and graceful. There is nothing extreme or overdone—just thoroughly dignified. They are cars such as the best citizens, persons of good judgment and refined taste will be proud to own. Their beauty is a type dictated, not by passing fancy, but by a desire for permanent attractiveness.[1]

Critics of those first Lincolns, on the other hand, regarded them as hopelessly stodgy, but they were typical of the quality car in the early years of the century. Neither Henry Ford nor Henry Leland, nor many automobile pioneers in between, gave much thought to aesthetic considerations in those days.

Also conspicuously absent from the discussion thus far is the medium-priced market segment, the last major segment to come into existence in recognizable form. This occurred after World War I and did so for several rea-

Alfred P. Sloan, who led General Motors for a quarter of a century
and helped define the medium-priced field.

sons. One was the astounding success of Henry Ford (and others) in extending automobile ownership to the masses of Americans. Prior to 1920, the vast
majority of new car sales were to first-time car buyers. Very few people had
ever bought a car twice. Inevitably, this game could only go on but so long;
sooner or later the pool of prospects who had never owned a car would di-
minish below the level required to keep the existing manufacturers in business. True, there would always be people entering the market for the first time,
but there would no longer be enough of them to keep the lines humming,
much less enough of them to fuel the continued growth of the industry.

The second reason for the development of the medium-priced market was
the nation's increasing prosperity. People had more money than ever before,
and as a result they were living better than ever before. There was a lot of dis-
posable income available for big-ticket items such as cars.

The third reason was Alfred Sloan. He was the man who, more than any
other single individual, figured out a way to deal with the problem of market
saturation, on the one hand, and how to get those increasingly prosperous
Americans to part with their money for new cars on a regular basis, on the
other. He figured all this out because it was the only way he could save his
company. In 1921, Sloan suddenly found himself running General Motors . . .
and it wasn't a pretty sight.

General Motors had been founded by William C. Durant. Together with the two Henrys—Leland and Ford—Durant was unarguably one of the central figures in the development of the automobile industry. It was his vision and energy that created General Motors and, as much as Henry Ford, transformed the industry into a major force in American life. Henry Ford's approach was to concentrate on a single, affordable car to the exclusion of everything else. Ford also ran his highly centralized company as a personal fiefdom, disdaining anything that even smacked of a modern industrial management organization. Durant, on the other hand, was one of the very first to understand—at least on some level—that the way to ultimate success was to blanket the market with a variety of brands. To do that required a highly complex organization that, unfortunately, was beyond Durant's management skills, but he was, at least, pointing in the right direction.

If Durant was a born builder who loved nothing better than creating great commercial enterprises, it seemed he couldn't help overdoing it. The chase was the important thing; once he had caught what he was after he didn't seem to know what to do next. He was—in the parlance of our own day—born to shop, and often he bought too well and none too wisely. His excesses invariably brought every automobile company he controlled to the brink of ruin. He went through this cycle twice with General Motors, losing control in 1910 and, again, in 1920. He repeated the process again with his own Durant Motors.

Moreover, Durant's mania for acquisition was facilitated, for the most part, with funny-money—stock trades, manipulations, speculations, and so forth—in the days when the securities markets were under very little government supervision or restraint. Durant created General Motors more-or-less with mirrors and mostly by juggling paper that otherwise hard-headed businessmen were willing to accept largely under the influence of the sheer force of his personality. He was able to get away with this because he was one of the greatest promoters in history. Walter Chrysler, who ran Buick for several years before going on to bigger things, provided the classic description of Durant:

> I cannot hope to find words to express the charm of the man. He has the most winning personality of anyone I've ever known. He could coax a bird right down out of a tree, I think.[2]

Unfortunately, the economy went into a minor depression in 1920, which hurt auto sales across the board, and Durant's stock speculations brought mighty General Motors to the brink of catastrophe. At that point, Pierre du Pont and Alfred Sloan were forced to take control to save the corporation from collapse, with du Pont organizing the financial bail-out and Sloan providing the day-to-day management skills.

General Motors was in a state of complete disarray insofar as its car divisions were concerned. There were no less than seven different divisions competing with ten model ranges, all but one of them (Cadillac) in competition with each other. And, none of them competing where the big volume was, in the low-priced field against Henry Ford's Model T. Moreover, a couple of the divisions were outright basket cases.

On April 6, 1921, a special committee at General Motors was organized by Sloan to investigate the situation within the corporation, define its basic purposes, and outline its future direction. It was in the course of this examination that Sloan began to formulate his concept of the automobile market as it had developed.

It seemed to Sloan that the automobile industry had experienced three major market cycles. These he called the "class market," the "mass market" and the "mass-class market."[3] In the earliest years of the industry, only the well-to-do could afford cars. This was the class market. After Henry Ford introduced his Model T, cars began to be built that were affordable for the masses of Americans, and this basic type of car soon took over the industry. This was the mass market. After World War I, however, increased prosperity, aided by the development of installment buying, induced many car buyers to raise their aspirations above the basic transportation level represented by the Model T. Thus, many of them were prospects for higher-priced cars of various descriptions. Many others, of course, still needed transportation of the cheapest type. This wide range of buyers constituted the mass-class market that, essentially, remains with us today.

Sloan was convinced that the existence of the new mass-class market strongly favored expansion of the medium-priced field. In fact, the share of new car sales going to the low-priced makes declined from well over 60 percent in 1920 to barely 40 percent by 1927. The Great Depression slowed this trend for a time, but did not stop it.

Sloan wasn't done though. In looking at the industry as it existed in 1921, he realized that the shift to the new mass-class market would hurt Henry Ford and be a boon to Henry Ford's competitors—if they were smart enough to take advantage of the opportunity. For Sloan, this was vital because Ford held such a strangle-hold on the industry at the time that real opportunity for the dozens of lesser auto makers could only come at Ford's expense. Change, Sloan reasoned, usually favors insurgents because they have less commitment, emotional and financial, to the status quo. Henry Ford was wedded—indeed, obsessively so, as events would demonstrate—to his Model T, and was determined to make no important changes in it, or even to supplement it with other models. The mass-class market, however, signified a rush to better grades of transportation; i.e., toward cars that, due to Henry Ford's intransigence, would not be Fords.

Moreover, Sloan intuitively understood that in this rapidly developing situation General Motors had one other advantage over its arch-rival and over the other insurgents, as well. Nearly all of the car companies were, in his word, "static." In other words, they built one car line in one price range. General Motors, as much by virtue of Durant's whims as by design, was "fluid."[4] General Motors was attempting—although, admittedly, with mixed success—to sell a number of different lines in a variety of price segments. As car buyers moved away from the basic level of transportation represented by the Model T, variety would be foremost on their minds. It stood to reason that the manufacturer that offered the greatest variety would stand to gain the most, and that manufacturer could be General Motors if Sloan and his cohorts could clean up the mess in time.

As a corollary to the above, Sloan was beginning to realize that those Model T owners who might be persuaded to want something a little better—i.e., a Chevy for a few dollars more—might, in time, become dissatisfied with their Chevy and want something better still. Extending this thought to its logical conclusion, General Motors could become the car company for millions of Americans, who would move up or down the price scale as need or desire dictated without ever leaving the General Motors family. A young man buying a Chevy might be expected to become more prosperous in time and move on up through the ranks to an Oldsmobile, then to a Buick, and, ultimately, even to a Cadillac. Chevrolet would have millions of customers who would never want anything better, of course, but the division would also cultivate hundreds of thousands of customers for Olds and Buick. It could work the other way, too. A certain number of well-to-do Buick households might need a less expensive second car, in which case Olds or Chevy would reap the benefits.

Eventually, Sloan's committee decided that General Motors should compete across the board within the industry, avoiding only the ultra-high-priced market where very few sales were made. They further identified six distinct price steps within the overall market where competitive car lines should be positioned:

    (a) $450–600
    (b) $600–900
    (c) $900–1,200
    (d) $1,200–1,700
    (e) $1,700–2,500
    (f) $2,500–3,500

Every price step would have what Sloan called "gravitational pull" on the price steps above and below it. In other words, the $600–900 car should be sufficiently attractive that it could draw customers up from the $450–600 step (those who wanted a better car), and down from the $900–1,200 step (those who wanted better value). That was how Chevrolet planned to attack Ford— by offering a better car for a few more dollars—and there was no reason the car priced just above Chevy wouldn't exert the same pull on Chevy's customer base.

It would require tremendous organizational skills to manage a complex empire such as Sloan envisioned, but it could be done. And, as it turned out, Sloan was just the man to do it. In an interview published in 1926—one of the few he ever granted—Sloan described his views on industrial organization. Although he didn't say so point blank, it is clear he was contrasting his views with those of Henry Ford:

> In modern, large-scale industry there are two major forms of organization: centralized and decentralized.
>
> If General Motors were to be centralized, we would have one man in supreme charge of all sales, another in supreme charge of engineering, another in supreme charge of manufacturing, and so forth.
>
> We are organized on a decentralized plan. Each operation, like Buick, Cadillac, Chevrolet, Oakland [later Pontiac], or Olds car or G.M.C. Truck, is headed by the best man we can find for that job, and he is charged with full responsibility for the success of that entire organization. In this way we develop greater initiative, greater enthusiasm and a greater sense of responsibility.[5]

Sloan then went on to describe succinctly why the decentralized General Motors system offered a critical advantage over the centralized, Ford-type system in the maturing automotive market of the 1920s:

> Talking of initiative, there is more room in the automotive industry than in most other industries—steel, for example—for originality. To the consumer of steel it doesn't make much difference who makes it. The automobile buyer, however, takes a different attitude. There is always a keen demand for originality.[6]

Yet, Henry Ford was determined to continue manufacturing cars exactly the same way the steel barons made steel—one size fits all. It was about as far removed from the Sloan concept—and from reality in the 1920s—as one could possibly get.

By 1925, the Sloan price-step plan had been enacted and General Motors was in far better competitive shape than it had been four years earlier. The price-step theory of marketing had even been embodied in a slogan which General Motors used for several years: "A Car for Every Purse and Purpose."

There were, however, two price steps left uncovered: between Chevy and Olds on the low end, and between Buick and Cadillac at the top. As early as 1923, Sloan had begun pushing the programs that would eventually result in filling these two identifiable gaps in the General Motors range. These programs ultimately resulted in the creation of the Pontiac in 1926, as a companion to Oakland, and the La Salle in 1927, as a companion to Cadillac.

Of the two price gaps, the gap between Chevy and Olds was clearly the most troubling to Sloan. In order to build up volume with Chevy and gain the manufacturing economies necessary to ultimately match Ford on price, Chevy could not be left vulnerable to a competitive product just above it that could steal sales, hence volume, from it. If, on the other hand, Sloan reasoned, the car just above Chevy were a General Motors product using many Chevy components, that car line would not only protect General Motors from outside competition, but could actually improve Chevy's volume efficiency. Sloan later recalled his thinking:

> From the strategic standpoint at that time the most dangerous gap in the list was that between the Chevrolet and the Olds. It was big enough to constitute a volume demand and thereby to accommodate, on top of Chevrolet, a competitor against whom we then had no counter. On this reasoning, we made one of the most important decisions in the history of General Motors, namely to fill the gap above Chevrolet with a brand-new car with a new six-cylinder engine. We had come to believe from an engineering standpoint that the future favored sixes and eights. However, to make the strategy effective, it would be necessary to fill the gap with a car that also had some volume economies. Otherwise, because the new car would draw some volume away from Chevrolet, reducing its economies, a loss would result for both cars. We concluded, therefore, that the new car must be designed in physical co-ordination with Chevrolet so as to share Chevrolet's economies, and vice versa.[7]

What Sloan was proposing was far more radical than it sounds. Up to that time, all manufacturers—including the semi-autonomous companies that comprised General Motors' automotive divisions—used their own bodies, chassis, engines, and so forth. It was a given that a more costly car, even if built by the same manufacturer, should have its own unique components. The concept of building two lines of cars in two different price categories using shared components—much less sharing components between brands— simply had not occurred to anyone. Or, if it had, the idea had been dismissed as unworkable, as heresy. So, what Sloan had in mind was more than just a new car line to plug a gap in the General Motors range; he was intent upon demonstrating that it was possible to share components across price ranges in order to improve the volume efficiency of the corporation as a whole. It was a daring concept with vast long-term implications for General Motors and for the industry.

The Sloan plan posed another problem, though. If Chevy and Pontiac shared substantial numbers of components, how could the Pontiac be made sufficiently more desirable to command a higher price from significant numbers of new car buyers? Once again, Sloan himself had accurately identified the course of the market in the 1920s and suggested the answer. As all cars in similar price classes became pretty much equally reliable and durable, Sloan predicted, it would no longer be possible to rely upon such factors to sell cars. Translation: engineering excellence was a declining asset in a market in which General Motors' main challengers were at least roughly competitive. But, the opposite was also probably true: within limits, shared engineering between brands was no longer a negative factor. In the mass-class market, buyers would inevitably turn their attention to non-essentials, such as comfort, beauty, novel features, or prestige. Indeed, that realization was a key reason General Motors developed Art and Colour, the industry's first in-house professional styling department in 1927.[8] Another manifestation of this trend was a prestige "cylinder war" that swept the industry. Chevrolet introduced a six in 1929 because Ford had a four. In 1932, Ford would introduce a V8 because Chevrolet had a six. And, so it went.

Try as he might, though, Henry Ford couldn't beat Sloan at his own game. General Motors' success with Sloan's marketing concepts was stunning. In 1922, the first year in which reliable industry-wide statistics were compiled, General Motors' market share stood at 18.5 percent. By 1927, it reached 42.5 percent and topped 47 percent in 1941, the last year before the outbreak of World War II. By contrast, Ford dropped from 48 percent of the market in 1922, to 18.8 percent in the same period. It was a complete role reversal.

Henry Ford's problems were compounded in this period by the arrival on the scene of Chrysler Corporation. After a highly successful career at General Motors, Walter P. Chrysler had taken early retirement from the presidency of Buick in 1920. He was lured back to the industry when the New York bankers needed someone to save Willys-Overland in 1921. So successful was Chrysler that he was begged to work the same magic on faltering Maxwell-Chalmers. This time, Chrysler decided to stick around and, by 1925, Maxwell-Chalmers had been transformed into Chrysler Corporation.

At first, the Chrysler was the only brand offered, having supplanted both Maxwell and Chalmers, but Walter Chrysler had watched Sloan's achievements at General Motors and learned the lessons well. In 1926, the Chrysler

Walter P. Chrysler.

Imperial was launched. Then in 1928, Chrysler executed a triple-play that left industry observers gasping with admiration. First Dodge, the largest of the independent manufacturers—and considerably larger even than Chrysler Corporation—was acquired through a brilliant stock trade. Almost at the same time, the low-priced Plymouth and medium-priced De Soto brands were launched. Overnight, Chrysler had come of age as a full-line auto producer and, now, Henry Ford was confronted by, not one, but two, huge competitors who spanned the price spectrum and were determined to aggressively exploit the new marketing realities.

Most industry observers and enthusiasts alike are accustomed to thinking of Chrysler as the number three auto producer, and generally a poor third, at that. It was not always so. In 1936, Chrysler became the number two automaker, having passed Ford as Henry Ford began to fall out of touch with developments in the industry. By 1941, Chrysler held a 24.1 percent market share, Ford a mere 18.8 percent. General Motors and Chrysler between them controlled over 70 percent of the market, and they had achieved that daunting penetration largely on the strength of their medium-priced lines. General Motors had three: Pontiac, Oldsmobile, and Buick. Chrysler also had three: Dodge, De Soto, and Chrysler. These medium-priced brands together commanded nearly 40 percent of the entire market—or, almost as much as Ford Motor Company's market share during its peak in the early 1920s.

If Henry Ford hadn't seen it coming, there were those within Ford Motor

Company who had. His son Edsel was one. His national sales manager, Jack Davis, was another. By the mid-1930s, both came to realize the brilliance of the way General Motors and Chrysler were operating, in terms of both their modern management organizations and their marketing strategies. Edsel Ford and Jack Davis also understood that, as a result, Ford's customer base was hemorrhaging. When Ford customers wanted to move up, the only option they had was to leave the Ford fold. As a practical matter, that meant Ford was cultivating customers for Pontiac, Oldsmobile, Buick, Dodge, De Soto, and Chrysler. They also realized that when the country eventually came out of its economic depression, the greatest growth potential would be in the medium-priced field. So, the problem would only get worse. Clearly, something had to be done.

In fact, something had been done, if only a comparative drop in the bucket. As was noted earlier in this book, in order to save Lincoln Edsel Ford had launched the Lincoln-Zephyr in 1936. Priced opposite the most expensive Buicks and Chryslers, it sold in large numbers for a Lincoln and succeeded in saving that division, but scarcely put a dent in total sales in the medium-priced field. Worse, it used its own body and chassis distinct from other Ford offerings. There was nothing resembling the standardized body programs by then instituted at General Motors and Chrysler. Ford, Lincoln-Zephyr, and Lincoln lines had virtually nothing in common except the Ford dealer network.

The company still needed a high-volume entry, and it needed it urgently. So Edsel laid plans for the car that became the Mercury, a car that was to be positioned solidly in the high-volume Pontiac-Dodge segment. A total of 65,884 Mercurys were built during 1939, its first full calendar year. That put it at a little more than 5 percent of overall production in the medium-priced field. If it was hardly enough to halt mid-market successes at General Motors and Chrysler, it was a respectable maiden effort—and long overdue. It is impossible to say how well the Mercury would have established itself under normal conditions, for World War II brought civilian passenger car production at all manufacturers to a halt almost as soon as the 1942 models were announced. It would be three-and-a-half years before volume production started up again and, by then, the auto industry—and Ford Motor Company—would be facing challenges no one had foreseen.

CHAPTER FOUR

A young Henry Ford II mixes with workers in 1945.

Prologue to the Edsel

BY THE END OF THE WAR, both Henry and Edsel Ford were gone, the latter having died in 1943, the former having been forced into retirement by the Ford family in September, 1945. The new president, Edsel's son Henry Ford II, faced a mess even worse than the one Sloan had confronted in 1921. Both companies had been in dreadful disarray, but Sloan's challenge was essentially strategic—one of reorganizing and rationalizing reasonably competent divisions, products, and personnel so that they pulled together toward well-conceived corporate goals—i.e., Sloan's problem was taking Durant's accumulated mess of car companies and making sense out of them.

Henry Ford II was handed next to nothing. Nearly all the good executives had been forced out of the company during his grandfather's tragic final years. There was no corporate organization plan worthy of the name, not even a bad one. Engineering and finance staffs, for example, were virtually non-existent. Product planning was a joke and the styling staff was embryonic. Plants and facilities were in turmoil. The Mercury brand had never had time to establish itself, Lincoln was struggling to maintain a luxury image, and only the Ford brand had any measurable residue of popular appeal—and that was waning.

Like Sloan in 1921, however, Henry II had an unwitting accomplice. Just as

Sloan had counted heavily on the inability of Ford Motor Company to rise to the marketing challenge of the 1920s, so Henry II was to benefit mightily from the collapse of Chrysler Corporation in the post-World War II era.

Chrysler, under the conservative leadership of K. T. Keller, who succeeded Walter Chrysler upon the latter's death in 1940, was falling farther and farther out of touch. To cite but one example, Chrysler, with one of the best engineering staffs in the world, stoutly resisted the increasingly popular automatic transmission, regarding it as a passing fad. At first, Ford Motor Company had neither the engineering depth nor the financial resources to develop one, either, but suitable units were soon sourced from outside suppliers.[1] Worse, the new 1949 Chrysler models were so painfully conservative in their styling that it became increasingly harder to move them even in the seller's market of the early postwar period.

Almost immediately upon assuming the helm, Henry II decided that the only way to resurrect Ford Motor Company was to emulate the General Motors model. That meant following both the General Motors organizational structure and the General Motors marketing strategy insofar as it was possible to do so. Significantly, one of his first major decisions was to hire Ernest R. Breech, then being groomed to succeed Sloan. In July, 1946, Breech was named to be the new executive vice-president of Ford Motor Company. In fact, Breech was brought in to perform the dual function of being a mentor to young Henry and to run the company on a day-to-day basis.

Breech, in turn, hired away many General Motors executives for a variety of top positions at Ford Motor Company. Notable among them were Lewis D. Crusoe, Harold Youngren, and Earle S. MacPherson. Youngren and MacPherson were engineers to whom was delegated the daunting challenge of building a credible engineering staff and bringing Ford products up to contemporary standards. Crusoe was a manager and hard-nosed finance man who was designated as Breech's chief assistant. In short order, Henry I's deliberate chaos gave way to the beginnings of a modern organizational structure. Well-defined staffs were created for finance, engineering, manufacturing, sales, purchasing, and industrial (labor) relations. Wags began to call Ford Motor Company the "Ford Division of General Motors," but they couldn't deny that Henry II was serious about learning General Motors' proven methods and applying them to his own troubled company.[2]

Henry II also hired a group of ten former Army Air Force officers.[3] Nearly all graduates of prestigious business schools, they had acted as advisors to the military during the war in precisely those areas in which Ford Motor Company was so desperately lacking: statistical analysis, cost-benefit analysis, cost

Ernest R. Breech.

controls, and so on. Ford met the group, investigated their resumés, and hired them in toto. They were immediately turned loose on an unsuspecting company, where they amazed and bewildered old-timers by asking an apparently endless series of questions of nearly everyone they met in an effort to get to know the place. As a result, they were quickly nicknamed the "Quiz Kids," after a popular juvenile radio program of the day. Eventually, as their success and power within the company grew to mythical proportions, the nickname evolved into the "Whiz Kids."

The Whiz Kids were headed by Charles "Tex" Thornton, and included Wilbur R. Anderson, Charles E. Bosworth, J. Edward Lundy, Robert S. McNamara, Arjay R. Miller, Ben D. Mills, George Moore, Francis C. "Jack" Reith, and James O. Wright. Thornton and Anderson left after a few months, and Thornton eventually founded Litton Industries. The rest of The Whiz Kids stayed and slowly began to infiltrate the company, then expand their control in it, using the financial staff as their power base. McNamara and Miller eventually rose to the presidency, while Lundy, as chief financial officer for many years in the 1960s and 1970s, was said by many insiders to be the most powerful man in the company. Reith, for his part, was to play a crucial role in conceptualizing the Edsel automobile.

Meaningful financial controls were certainly in desperate want at Ford Motor Company in 1946. In one department under the old regime, costs were estimated by weighing stacks of invoices. (The average cost of a certain quantity of invoices had been calculated at one point in time, and, thereafter, all the invoices that came in were stacked and weighed.) There were no serious profit-and-loss records for the company's diverse operations. No one really knew what it cost to build a car. At the end of the year, the money expended was deducted from the money taken in and that was the profit. Or loss— which came to be the normal state of affairs by the end of the war.

Without cost controls, it was nearly impossible to weed out the losers and improve the winners and, by 1946, Ford Motor Company was losing an estimated $10 million per month. There can be little doubt that the Whiz Kids were able to make a critical contribution very quickly. The company was divided up into profit centers, the chronic losers were given the axe (such as the rubber plantation in Brazil, which had been one of the Old Man's pet projects and had never earned a dime), and financial health was soon restored.

In a sense, though, there was less there than met the eye. The results at Ford Motor Company were not atypical of what happens when "bean counters" take control of a badly mismanaged company. It is remarkably easy, in such circumstances, to show significant improvements in a short period of time simply by instituting sensible cost controls. Part of the problem is that product people often show too little concern for the bottom line and, as Sloan well understood, someone in authority has to be in a position to count—and, ultimately, control—the beans.

The problem with financial types, though, is that they often have little feel for the product. To them, statistical analysis is often the only sensible way to plan anything, products included. But, again, as Sloan understood, customers don't buy statistical analyses. They buy cars, and they make their buying decisions based on factors—such as reputation, value, prestige, driving characteristics, and appearance—that defy quantification. The automobile business is one of the most intuitive on earth, and more than one car company has been seriously damaged by bean counters run amok. Unfortunately, the damage the bean counters do when they gain too much control—unlike the quick benefits they can produce at first—can take years, or even decades, to become obvious.[4]

True to form, the Whiz Kids, for all their talent, had little feel for, or appreciation of, automobiles. They could just as well have been selling aluminum siding, and, in fact, Ford Motor Company was only one of several firms in various industries to whom they had offered their services. Robert McNamara, who eventually became the leader of the group, was a man universally described by associates as possessing not only towering ambition but awesome brilliance when it came to numbers. He was also widely regarded as a man who had absolutely no love for cars, perhaps even found them a little distasteful. Of all The Whiz Kids, only Jack Reith was said to have any special fondness for the products the company was building. To McNamara and the others, the statistical reports they churned out with increasing sophistication (and used so skillfully to solidify their control) *were* the company. The cars rolling off the final assembly lines were, to them, almost incidental.[5]

The Whiz Kids had signed on thinking that they would (at least within a short period of time) run the company. The hiring of Breech prompted a confrontation of sorts, and proved to be the harbinger of confrontations to come. Thornton, on behalf of his group, demanded that Henry II sign a paper vesting all authority for corporate planning in them. When Breech heard about it, he told Henry that if such was the case, he (Breech) wasn't needed. Henry sided with Breech and Thornton left soon afterward, but it was an ominous portent.

Some biographers have written that the main appeal of The Whiz Kids to

The "Whiz Kids" in a photo taken on June 28, 1946. *Front row, left to right,* Arjay Miller, Francis C. Reith, George Moore, James O. Wright, Charles B. "Tex" Thornton, W. R. Anderson, Charles E. Bosworth, Ben D. Mills, J. Edward Lundy, and Robert S. McNamara.

Henry II was that they, unlike other executives within the company, were close to his own age. Others have suggested that Ford kept them around because they acted as a counterweight against the Breech faction whose knowledge and expertise, however much it was needed, Ford found threatening. Whatever the reason, the practical (though probably unintended) effect was to lay the groundwork for competing factions within the company that would lead to major rifts and clashes as the Whiz Kids grew in power and influence in the 1950s. The gaping chasm that separated the bean counters from the product people was to have a profound influence on the postwar development of the company—and on the Edsel program.

Richard Stout, who was a member of Lincoln-Mercury product planning off-and-on from 1950 to 1966, notes that empire building was by no means confined to the financial side:

> Earle MacPherson was building his central engineering department into an empire that was not going to relinquish any of its jewels, no matter where they might rightly or strategically belong. Under the umbrella of reorganization, power bases could be insidiously formed, and empire building was a surreptitious by-product. Finance, engineering, and manufacturing had already built bastions. Creating great automobiles seemed to have secondary importance in this context.[6]

Ford was destined to out-do General Motors in at least one respect: it became the most "political" of the car companies—for good or for ill. But, all that was in the future. At the time, the company seemed to be well on the road to recovery. A modern organizational plan was being instituted under the direction of Breech and Crusoe. The Whiz Kids had developed meaningful cost controls, divided the company into well-defined profit centers, and were giving Breech the hard data he needed to plan for future expansion. That expansion would be two-fold. It would involve reinvigorating the Ford brand, on the one hand, and turning Mercury and Lincoln into serious competitors in their respective price classes, on the other.

As early as 1947, Henry II had recognized his company's weakness in the medium-priced field. Mercury and Lincoln were split off from the Ford franchise and the new Lincoln-Mercury Division was created with his younger brother, Benson, at the helm. The effort was prompted mainly by a recognized need to get the Mercury brand far enough away from the Ford that it could develop its own identity. It was assumed at Lincoln-Mercury that this was merely the first step in an eventual establishment of separate Mercury and Lincoln divisions.

Bob Gregorie, who had left the company in the aftermath of Edsel Ford's death, returned within the year to act as chief designer of the 1949 postwar Ford, Mercury, and Lincoln lines. Significantly, Mercury would no longer use the Ford body shell. It and the medium-priced Lincoln—the successor to the Zephyr—would share a new mid-sized body, while a full-bore luxury Lincoln—the Cosmopolitan—would give that brand a credible presence in the top-end of the market for the first time in years. A 1949 Continental was proposed, but never really had much of a chance. For one thing, it just didn't look right on the slab-sided 1949 Cosmopolitan body. For another, its chief patron, Edsel Ford, was no longer alive. (Gregorie was gone, too, after George Walker was selected to style the 1949 Fords.)

The most important reason the Continental was dropped, however, was that—for the first time—each individual product line was subjected to cost analysis. On the basis of that analysis, slow-selling, low-profit (or, in some cases, no-profit) models were dropped so that the company could concentrate on the high-volume, high-profit ones. On the surface, this move was long overdue. On a deeper level, though, it posed problems and demonstrated that the new Ford team had not learned all the lessons General Motors had to offer.

It is unlikely, for example, that the prewar Lincoln Continental or Custom (the limousines) had ever turned a profit, nor is it likely that Edsel Ford cared. It was not that he wanted to lose money, but he realized (as did Sloan at General Motors) that sometimes you had to lose money in order to make money. Particularly in the Lincoln price class, people bought cars for highly subjective reasons, such as prestige. It was vital to have high-visibility models that would draw attention to the rest of the line. In the auto industry, this is called the "halo" effect, and it is absolutely vital to the success of a luxury brand. As a practical matter, prestige was often promoted by the very models that—on the books, at any rate—were financial disasters. The need for "halo" models was the reason Sloan allowed Cadillac to build a money-losing V16 series at the depths of the Depression and it was the reason Edsel built the Continental. Looked at in broad terms, they didn't really lose money because the attention and prestige created by these "losers" sold many a standard Cadillac and Lincoln in the 1930s and 1940s—cars that would not have been sold without the reflected glow the "halo" models provided. Because the "halo" effect was highly intuitive, and, therefore, beyond statistical analysis, however, its importance was something the bean counter mindset had enormous trouble grasping.

One serious matter no one at Ford Motor Company had trouble grasping, though, was the deplorable state of the company's penetration in the medium-priced field. As early as 1948, Henry Ford II had suggested the need for the addition of a new mid-priced line and set up a committee to make recommendations. A particularly troubling study showed that 87 percent of Chevy owners traded up to the Pontiac-Olds-Buick trio, 77 percent of Plymouth owners traded up to the Dodge-De Soto-Chrysler trio, but only 26 percent of Ford owners traded up to Mercury. Groused Crusoe, "We have been growing customers for General Motors." Indeed, it was true.

In 1949, a plan was presented to the executive committee detailing this second line to Ford's medium-priced offerings. The plan proposed to create a new line to fill the entire medium-price class—consisting of four offerings to augment the current Mercury series—thus allowing the buyer a much larger selection. With the outbreak of war in Korea in the summer of 1950, however, this proposal was laid aside. Faced with the institution of government volume restrictions, price controls, and allocation of critical materials, it was simply impossible to consider launching any sort of serious expansion until the war was over.

In the meantime, attention was concentrated on the company's existing product lines. The all-new 1952 cars were being designed, engineered, and tooled. Ford and Mercury were to have had new, overhead-valve engines, but Korean War shortages forced their postponement. The rest of the Ford, Mercury, and Lincoln product plans went forward as scheduled, though, and there is every indication they were precisely what Earle MacPherson and Ford Motor Company's product planners wanted. To that extent, they were a cause of deepening concern within Lincoln-Mercury Division.

It was almost as if the Breech faction and Whiz Kids had conspired to squeeze the life out of the Lincoln-Mercury product program. The Whiz Kids, with their reams of statistical analyses, had made sure that the model line-ups were pared back to the irreducible minimum. Only the top-sellers survived the cut. That meant no special models were left to add zest to the brands. MacPherson, on the other hand, had forced both Mercury and Lincoln lines to be engineered in accord with his preference with lightweight, smaller cars. This was a problem in the new Mercury, which came out looking terribly plain, but it was a near disaster with the Lincoln.

In searching around for a benchmark upon which to base the 1952 Lincoln design, MacPherson had used the Oldsmobile 98—in other words, a car that was not even in the luxury class. Lincoln-Mercury executives were appalled. In a luxury market that was trending toward bigger, heavier, more powerful, and gaudier cars, the new Lincoln was smaller, economy-minded, and undistinguished. Indeed, the 1952 Lincolns were hard to distinguish from the Mercurys, despite the fact that the bodies were entirely different.[7]

Lincoln-Mercury's direct control over the final product was limited to superficial items such as color and trim, but, within those parameters, they went to work on the Lincoln with an air of desperation. In the end, the Lincoln was beautifully trimmed and—to give MacPherson credit where it is due—a remarkable road car. It was also, however, under-powered and far too small to be a hot competitor in the luxury class.

The frustration within Lincoln-Mercury mounted exponentially during the last few months prior to the announcement of the 1952 models. "Can't do business from an empty wagon" became a favorite gripe around the division.[8] Then, Emmet Judge, the division's chief product planner, stumbled across a way to fill the wagon.

CHAPTER FIVE

1949 Lincoln.

Learning Their ABCs

THE 1950 GENERAL MOTORS interchangeability program had been in production for nearly a year before anyone at Ford Motor Company realized what had been done. The man who spilled the beans was Richard Stout, who had recently joined the company after a stint with General Motors' design staff. When Stout's boss—Lincoln-Mercury Division's chief product planner, Emmet Judge—explained what had happened to top executives at Ford, the effect was very much like shouting "Fire!" in a crowded theater. Absolute pandemonium erupted . . . and the Edsel was the eventual result. What General Motors had developed was a startling new twist on its well-established program of sharing bodies between divisions.

The Great Depression had put enormous pressure on all car companies to reduce costs. The advent of the all-steel body at about the same time, with its requirement for tremendous up-front investment in tooling, posed another challenge. For General Motors, the combination was the clincher; the corporation could no longer afford not to share bodies. The 1933 A-body program for Chevy, Pontiac, and Olds, was the first serious interchangeability program at General Motors, and, by 1940, all volume product lines were built on a range of letter-designated body shells: A, B, and C. Moreover, these bodies were shared extensively, with as many as four divisions using a single body. Chrysler had pioneered the same bandwagon as early as 1929 when its De Soto and Plymouth brands first shared bodies, but it was not an easy "sell" within Ford Motor Company.

As late as 1939, as has been noted in previous chapters, Ford, Mercury, Lincoln-Zephyr, and Lincoln lines used essentially unique body shells. Ten years later there were still three: the small Ford body, the mid-size body used by Mercury and the standard Lincoln, and the large Lincoln body used exclusively by the Lincoln Cosmopolitan. Thus, only the mid-size body was shared between brands. The 1952 product lines, just about to enter production when Judge began his study of the General Motors program, reduced the body count to two: one shared by Ford and Mercury, and one as a Lincoln exclusive, with no interchangeability between them.

Ford planners knew that General Motors had a body interchangeability program in the medium- and high-priced fields, but they assumed that fundamental departures from theoretical interchangeability continued to exist. How else could General Motors build Oldsmobiles, Buicks, and Cadillacs that looked so distinctly different? The 1949–51 Mercury and Lincoln lines that

1949 Mercury, which shared the same body shell as the Lincoln on page 62.

shared the mid-size shell looked it. So did the 1952 Ford and Mercury. It was painfully obvious, as well, that Chrysler shared bodies up and down its model range; Plymouth, Dodge, De Soto, and Chrysler models were hard to tell apart at any distance by all but the most knowledgeable. Yet, that was the inevitable price you paid for true interchangeability, wasn't it?

General Motors had confronted the "me, too," styling problems associated with sharing bodies.[1] But, General Motors had also discovered the reverse, as well; i.e., that having unique bodies didn't necessarily make the different lines look distinct from one another. Charles S. Mott, head of the GM automotive divisions at the time the Pontiac was developed in the 1920s, later recalled:

> I wanted to use common bodies, but I couldn't get that across. . . . Fisher Body was making the bodies, so Red Fisher said, "Well, if you are going to get more money for it, then it should have a bigger body." That was against what I wanted to do. They built it and made all special tools, since they didn't want the car to look like a Chevrolet. Well, when at last they built the car, and had it at the [1926 New York auto] show in Lexington Avenue—on one side was the Chevrolet, and on the other was the Pontiac, but they had painted the two cars exactly the same and you would have sworn it was the same body. I would have used the same body, but painted the cars a different color.[2]

It was an idea that was occurring to others. Almost as soon as General Motors' original styling section, Art and Colour, was established in 1927, body drafts for all of the corporation's products were requested from Fisher Body. One of Harley Earl's senior designers, Vincent Kaptur, began comparing them and found, to his amazement, that in several cases two or three completely different bodies from different divisions were within an inch of each other in critical dimensions. He went to Earl and suggested using common bodies for similar products, but differentiating them through creative use of color and trim, and perhaps a few unique exterior panels. This was a seminal idea: that brand distinction derived more from ornamentation than it did from the basic body.

And it was true. When Frank Hershey copied the finned oil cooler on a Napier race car to give the 1935 Pontiac its "Silver Streaks," he created a styling signature as arresting as any body shape. Better still, any body shell Pontiac cared to use could be instantly made to look like a Pontiac simply by adding the distinctive thin chrome bars to the hood and rear deck. Soon, all of General Motors' automotive divisions sprouted styling signatures of their own: Buick had its aggressive vertical grille bars (or "teeth") and its "portholes" in the front fenders, Cadillac had its egg-crate grille and tail fins, and so on. By the 1940s, there was a distinctive "look" for every division from Chevrolet to Cadillac. Why Ford and Chrysler were so slow to pick up on this is one of the enduring mysteries of the industry.[3] The sophistication of the 1950 General Motors body program, on the other hand, carried the concept to unimagined heights and left all of its competitors in the dust, Ford especially. As Emmet Judge learned to his utter amazement, Olds, Buick, and Cadillac shared the same basic body! Although separate B, C, and D designations were used, every car from the B-body Buick Special to the imperious D-body Cadillac Seventy-Five limousine was built off some variation of that body at a savings of tens of millions of dollars to General Motors. In fact, what Stout had revealed was one of the cleverest product rationalization programs in industry history.

Indeed, the program of product rationalization begun at General Motors in the early 1930s came to full flower in this era. The goal was to have every General Motors division, except Chevrolet (which only had one body to start with), reduced to one basic body shell between 1949 and 1950. They actually came close to achieving that. Pontiac dropped from two to one. Buick and Cadillac went from three to one (or, four to one in Cadillac's case, depending on how body shells are interpreted). From 1949, Pontiac and Chevrolet shared the A-body. Olds used both the A-body and the larger B-body in 1950, and was the only exception to the one-body rule. Buick and Cadillac technically had B-, C-, and D-bodies in 1950, but the new C-body was a stretched derivative of the B-body. The C-Special used by the Cadillac Sixty Special was, in turn, an even lengthier version of the B/C-body. Even the Series Seventy-Five D-body was engineered off the B/C-body.[4]

The brilliance of the General Motors interchangeability scheme is perhaps best illustrated by the Seventy-Fives. The bean counters at Ford had decided to drop the long wheelbase Lincolns after the war, and no serious thought was given to reviving them as part of the 1949 or 1952 programs. The sales involved could not justify the costs for what would have to have been a unique (or nearly so) seven-passenger body. But, how much had the Seventy-Five series actually cost Cadillac? How much in it was really unique?

As Stout revealed, the rear fenders were borrowed from the Coupe de Ville, and virtually every other sheet metal component in the body was taken "off the shelf" from other Cadillacs. The rear doors and the roof were the only significant unique stampings—and the roof was originally cobbled together from the C-Special roof until it got too bothersome to do it that way and Cadillac opted for separate tooling. It was one of the slickest tricks ever, and set a standard for limousine design in the industry for years to come.

Why was General Motors so anxious to simplify its product lines? The answer was simple: cost. The corporation's management, still guided by the legendary Alfred Sloan, had been genuinely taken aback by the dramatic price

Top, a 1951 Cadillac Sixty Special; *bottom*, a 1951 Oldsmobile Ninety-Eight—
General Motors products that shared the same body shell.

inflation that occurred as soon as price controls were eased at the end of World War II. There were many in General Motors leadership—Sloan among them —who were haunted by the sharp recession that had followed the last world war. In that economic crisis, General Motors had come close to ruin. So, although there was a huge pent-up demand for cars in the first years after the war, Sloan and his colleagues knew that sooner or later supply would meet demand. When that happened buyers might react to the prices being charged. General Motors couldn't roll the clock back to 1942, but it could cut expenses to the bone by eliminating unnecessarily costly complexity in its product lines. General Motors would place its trust in the creativity of its design chief, Harley Earl, and his minions at the styling center to make sure the individual brands maintained their distinct identities.

In the B/C/D-body program, every extra dollar that was spent produced the maximum appearance change. For example, the C-body used by the top-end Buicks (the Super and Roadmaster) and the volume Cadillac (the Series Sixty-Two) was essentially a stretched B-body. The passenger compartment was where the stretch occurred, so the C-body had its own roof. Earl made sure that the C-body roof had a "six window" design (with quarter windows behind the rear doors) so that it was instantly distinguishable from the "four window" B-body cars. Exterior sheet metal, such as fenders, rear deck lids, and hoods differed between brands, of course, so Earl—taking advantage of an unavoidable expense—made sure each brand had its own proportions. The Buick hood and front fenders had to be longer than that of the Cadillac owing to Buick's longer, straight-eight engine, so Earl gave Cadillacs longer rear fenders and deck lids. Underneath, nearly all the hidden body parts were interchangeable, but the Buick and the Cadillac looked dramatically different.[5]

Emmet Judge was mesmerized by what he had learned and was determined that Ford Motor Company executives should be told about it. He also knew that words alone wouldn't adequately convey the brilliance of what he had discovered. So, given a flair for showmanship, he and Stout developed a clever visual demonstration that quickly became known around Lincoln-Mercury as the "paper doll" show. Cut-outs of the different components for all Olds, Buick, and Cadillac models using the B/C/D-body—fenders and hoods, roofs, doors, rear fenders, and deck lids—were prepared with magnetic backing so that Stout could literally build any variant right before the eyes of his audience. What better way to demonstrate the interchangeability? He could start with an Olds 98 and, by switching pieces on his board, build every B/C/D-body car from the Buick Special right up through the Cadillac Seventy-Five! Recalled Stout:

The GM Interchangeability Chart used in Lincon-Mercury's "paper doll" show.

To make applied parts stick better, magnets were put on the back of the boards, with small metal strips attached to the back of each part. This, unexpectedly, caused a "plopping" sound when the parts were applied to the board.[6]

Judge's paper doll show was a big hit at Lincoln-Mercury Division. Having long chafed under their inability to afford the complex product programs of their competitors, it came as a complete revelation. Perhaps Lincoln-Mercury could afford to play with the big boys after all. Morgan Collins, Lincoln-Mercury's controller, decided to put Judge's discovery to the test and actually "cost out" the General Motors B/C/D-body program. As he suspected, Collins found that the high-volume lines bore most of the cost. That made sense. Where low-volume models were involved, such as the Cadillac Seventy-Fives, the incremental cost was kept well within the incremental sales increase these models could be expected to produce. In other words, every Oldsmobile, Buick, and Cadillac model involved—no matter how high or low its volume—paid its own way.

In contrast, the Lincoln-Mercury program was a mess. Mercury and Lincoln, both new for 1952, used entirely separate bodies with no interchangeability at all. So, unlike Cadillac, Lincoln (which was selling a third as many cars, to boot) had to support the entire cost of a separate body program and still couldn't afford low-volume, high-prestige models such as limousines—or a replacement for the late, lamented Continental. As Morgan Collins calculated it, the amortized cost for the Lincoln's body tooling was six times what Olds, Buick, and Cadillac were spending, simply due to the lack of sophisticated interchangeability. The General Motors model program was one even a bean counter could love. In fact, Collins was so enthused he suggested that Lincoln-Mercury Division propose a program of their own similar to the B/C/D program. Recalled Stout:

> Emmet Judge was the mentor/guide/coach behind the project. Morgan Collins was the power. Benson Ford and Stanley Ostrander—who, in effect, was general manager of Lincoln-Mercury—had seen the General Motors presentation and were much interested in an L-M version.[7]

The plan quickly gathered steam within Lincoln-Mercury. By the time the proposal was ready, it included not only expanded Mercury and Lincoln product lines, but a new Mercury entry designed to plug the gap that existed between the two. By emulating the B/C/D program, Ford Motor Company could afford the equivalent of another entire brand for a total cost not much more than it was already spending on a product program that every one within the company realized was seriously deficient.

The portentous meeting at which Emmet Judge's B/C/D interchangeability show and the proposed Lincoln-Mercury program was presented to top Ford management occurred on August 15, 1951. Stout recalled the scene at Ford Motor Company headquarters:

> In the center of the yellow wood-paneled conference room was a large, U-shaped conference table. Henry II and Ernest Breech would sit mid-way down on one side, with Lincoln-Mercury brass directly across from them. Other vice-presidents and staff members would be scattered around the table. The podium, charts, and other material were just beyond the open end of the table. On the far wall at the other end of the room, portraits of old Henry and Edsel watched us closely. "Hi, Edsel," I said under my breath. "You could do this whole new car bit without any of this stuff. We sure need you. . . ."[8]

Henry Ford II never showed up. He had been "sent out to play golf," Stout remembered. This was an ominous sign. Even more ominous was the arrival of Breech:

Most of the committee was seated. In stormed "stocky, cocky Ernest Breech," as the press delighted to call him. All hell broke loose. . . . A tirade of excruciating language. What an entrance! When one could finally sort out what was going on, it was realized that Lincoln-Mercury was being castigated in no uncertain terms for taking matters into their own hands. Who do you (expletives deleted) think you are? Rocking Ford Motor Company at a time like this, you (expletives deleted)! Who do you think does planning around here? On and on it went. The language was purple as purple can get, with exquisite choice of expletives.

Like a Marine drill instructor, Breech was a master. Men used to bullying, cringed; others looked like bewildered raccoons. I was wide-eyed. Suddenly it stopped. Breech had the room in the palm of his hand. No one else was going to claw Lincoln-Mercury.

Pleasantly, he turned and said, "Go ahead Emmet."

Emmet Judge stepped up to the podium. I manned the General Motors interchangeability boards.

"Let's skip this part about General Motors," said Earle MacPherson. "We all know that already."

"I don't think we all do," said our Stanley Ostrander, pointedly. "I want you to see this."

"Go ahead," said Breech.[9]

After the spectacular beginning, the presentation seemed to go well. Everyone was amused by the "plopping" sound the parts made and demanded that Stout show them how it was done. Breech seemed particularly interested in the Lincoln-Mercury Division program. In short, the day had turned into a glorious high for Lincoln-Mercury Division personnel, who congratulated themselves all the way back to their offices. Recalled Stout:

Returning to [Lincoln-Mercury] division headquarters at Warren and Livernois, there were more congratulations and a feeling of relief and joy. "Wasn't that fun!" exclaimed Morgan Collins. It was; it was great fun. Stanley Ostrander, who did not believe in compliments, expressed unrestrained pleasure. Benson was delighted. The long, circuitous journey to the Edsel car had begun.[10]

Then, a few days later, McNamara and the other Whiz Kids asked for a private showing. It was duly provided and courteously received. The next day, the word came down to Lincoln-Mercury Division from on high that their little show was never to be given again. The identity of the person or persons who gave the order has been lost to history, but the reason was that Ford Motor Company had been thrown into absolute turmoil.

Lincoln-Mercury had, it seemed, unwittingly trampled on quite a few sensitive toes. Among the owners of those toes was the company's chief engineer, Earle MacPherson, who was livid to have someone—anyone—try to usurp his authority to plan products for the divisions. Old Lincoln-Mercury hands still insist that MacPherson wreaked his revenge by delaying the next scheduled Lincoln body change by a year from 1955 to 1956.

Perhaps more worrisome, at least as events would unfold, was that the Whiz Kids, led by Robert McNamara, were also incensed. They, too, had staked out corporate planning as their private preserve and had taken to reacting ferociously if anyone planned anything important without their input. Already they were having serious conflicts over allocation of company resources with the Breech faction (which included MacPherson)—and were starting to win more than a few—but this was a development that caught them totally off guard.

The one thing that the McNamara and Breech factions could tacitly agree on was that there was no room at Ford Motor Company for anyone else to try to call the shots. On the other hand, the Lincoln-Mercury plan had been so

A 1952 Lincoln Capri.

well-thought-out, and the need so compelling, that it couldn't be ignored. Indeed, that was a large part of what angered the Breech and McNamara factions; i.e., there was a genuine crisis afoot, and someone else had spotted it and come up with a plausible solution first. So, they resorted to one of the time-honored defensive strategies of threatened bureaucrats everywhere: They called for another committee to study the matter all over again.

In January, 1952, Henry II appointed Jack Davis, the corporate vice-president of sales, to head this new committee. Its membership was restricted to the Breech faction, including Davis and Lewis Crusoe. The Whiz Kids weren't represented, nor was Lincoln-Mercury Division. The Davis committee's mission was to examine possible ways the company could establish a greater presence in the medium-priced field. Two months later, the committee's report was published in a massive six-volume set intended for high-level internal distribution. The "Davis Book" recommended:

- A new brand would be established by clever interchangeability. The Ford-Mercury body shell would remain, but a larger version of the Mercury sharing Lincoln body components would fill the gap between Mercury and Lincoln. This new car was dubbed the "Mercury-Monterey" and was intended to be strictly a Mercury

A 1952 Mercury, not sharing the same body shell as the Capri, but looking as if it did.

project. It would be a hyphenated Mercury, and would be sold,
initially at least, through existing Mercury outlets. In time, it could
be developed into a Monterey brand in its own right and split off
from Mercury. This was much the same plan that had been used
successfully in the launch of the original Mercury in 1939.

- The standard Mercury would be moved up slightly in its price point
  to separate it more from the Ford line.

- A new, ultra-luxury car in the Continental tradition would be
  developed by a new Special Products Division.

- Ford Motor Company would be expanded to four automotive
  divisions: Ford, Mercury, Lincoln, and Special Products.[11]

The Davis committee recommendations were accepted in part—all except
for the core of the report concerning the medium-priced field, which had
been the reason for the exercise in the first place. The Special Products Division was headed by William Clay Ford, Henry's youngest brother, and work
was begun that eventually resulted in the Continental Mark II. The Mercury
product range was not moved up even slightly in price (relative to Ford), nor
was Lincoln-Mercury split into two divisions. As for the Mercury-Monterey,
it was sent down to Lincoln-Mercury Division for further study. Emmet
Judge and Richard E. Krafve (pronounced "kraffy"), the recently appointed
assistant general manager, were named to direct the effort. Krafve was later
described by one industry observer as a "forceful" man with "a habitually puzzled look." As it turned out, he would have much to be puzzled about.

In October, 1952, the Judge-Krafve report was ready. Titled, "The 1956
Monterey Lincoln Program," the report gave detailed recommendations for
the Monterey (unhyphenated by this point). Essentially, the Monterey com-
bined a lighter version of the Lincoln body with Mercury mechanical components. It would be sold, at least at first, through Lincoln-Mercury dealers.

So, Ford Motor Company had now been blessed with three eminently
workable plans for a much-needed expansion in the medium-priced field: the
Lincoln-Mercury plan devised by Emmet Judge and Morgan Collins; the Davis plan; and the Judge-Krafve plan. For more than a year, top executives were
so busy attending meetings to prepare plans, to discuss plans, even to discuss
whether to discuss plans, that Ford Motor Company became known internally as the Ford Meeting Company. And, out of it all came . . . nothing. In
the best bureaucratic tradition, none of the plans were rejected outright, but
all were allowed to die a natural death. Then, silence descended over the company for more than two years.

The lack of activity did not, however, mean that powerful people within the company had given up the idea. To the contrary. With the stubbornness of a bunch of drunks who look for trouble until they find it, as one observer later put it, yet another plan was quietly set in motion. In the early months of 1955, rumors began to circulate through the company that a new brand would soon be developed for the medium-priced field.

And this, as the dime novels say, is where the plot thickens. . . .

CHAPTER SIX

Jack Reith in a 1957 Mercury, the pace car at the Indianapolis 500.

The Plot Thickens

FORD MOTOR COMPANY had made dramatic strides since the elevation of Henry Ford II to the presidency in 1945. From a dismal—and declining—18.8 percent of the market and third place status in 1941 (the last full year before the war stopped production), the company had risen to 30.8 percent in 1954 and a solid second place behind General Motors. Chrysler Corporation had been passed in 1950, and, by 1954, was down to its lowest market share since 1931. Now, the energetic team in Dearborn was setting its sights on mighty General Motors.

Already, the Ford brand was making heroic gains in the low-priced field. Ford may even have overtaken Chevrolet for first place in sales in that high-volume market segment—depending on whether you believed the company's press releases on the subject. Auto company advertising copy writers and public relations officials were master "spin doctors" long before that term entered the political lexicon. Especially in close sales contests, two or three competing brands might claim to be "first" by juggling the figures, but, according to the most reliable industry statistics for calendar year 1954, Chevrolet managed to hold onto its premier position—barely. Chevy officially registered 1,417,453 cars nationwide to Ford's 1,400,440. Nevertheless, the contest was closer than it had been in twenty years—virtual parity, in fact—and convinced everyone at the company that they were finally on a roll.

Indeed, it seemed to be true. Yet, there remained a couple of nagging problems to be resolved before General Motors could be toppled: Mercury and Lincoln. Despite the expenditure of vast sums since the war, Lincoln struggled along in the doldrums. Still, the company had laid energetic plans to remedy the situation, with the Continental Mark II and a dramatically new standard Lincoln in the pipeline for 1956. The solution had yet to be found, though, for the company's tepid performance in the lucrative medium-priced field.

The Mercury had made a respectable, if limited, place for itself in industry sales by 1950—and was doing better than double the prewar pace—but then had reached a plateau. Mercury's share of sales in the medium-priced field, specifically, in 1954, amounted to only 12.6 percent. In contrast, General Motors accounted for 59.6 percent (Pontiac, Oldsmobile, and Buick). Even Chrysler Corporation, despite its near collapse as a co-equal partner in the Big Three, managed somehow to hold onto a 15.5 percent share (Dodge, De Soto, and Chrysler).

Henry II was upset because he knew that his long-range goal of making the family business first again in the industry could not be achieved on the basis of low-priced sales alone. The product men around him were concerned, as well. This group included most of the men who still called the shots at the company: among them were Ernie Breech, the executive vice-president, Lewis Crusoe, the head of Ford Division, and Jack Davis, the vice-president for sales.

In January, 1955, Breech was promoted to the chairmanship and his old job was divided into two new positions: Crusoe became vice-president in charge of the car and truck group and head of all product planning, while Delmar S. Harder (another Breech loyalist) became vice-president in charge of manufacturing. The round of promotions also included a signal victory for The Whiz Kids: Robert McNamara, the group's unofficial leader, was named to head Ford Division. The rest of the Whiz Kids were moving up, as well, most notably Arjay Miller, who was company controller (chief financial officer), and Jack Reith, who was scoring a huge success as head of the company's troubled subsidiary in France. The growing power of the Whiz Kids encouraged them to challenge the Breech group more and more often, with the company becoming increasingly factionalized as a result. The finance-types and the product men, as has been noted in previous chapters, are rarely allies in the auto business, but few major car companies had ever dared give their bean counters so much power.

Reith, however, was an anomaly. Although he was a bona fide Whiz Kid,

Lewis Crusoe.

he also had a feel for cars. Unlike most of the others in his group, he actually seemed to like them. This made him one of the few top executives in the company who felt comfortable in both camps. In particular, Lewis Crusoe had come to admire and respect him, and Crusoe's power was considerable. It was shortly after Reith returned to Detroit to take a staff job under Crusoe that rumors of the company's impending new entry into the medium-priced field began to circulate.

For his part, Crusoe was an enormously well-liked figure in the company. Slight of build and dapper of attire, Crusoe was "Uncle Louie" to a generation of company executives. The Ford Division had scored its great postwar recovery largely under his leadership, including the launching of the two-seater Thunderbird. The T-Bird got mixed reviews within the company—some dismissed it as combining the discomfort of a sports car with the tepid performance of a family sedan—but it did wonders for Ford Division's image. It was, in fact, a perfect "halo" model, much as the original Continental had been for Lincoln.

With Crusoe's elevation to the group vice-presidency, he was able to turn his sights on the problem of expansion in the medium-priced field. Ford and Chevy were each taking roughly 25 percent of the market overall, the highly successful General Motors "B-O-P" lines (Buick-Olds-Pontiac) were taking roughly 25 percent, and everyone else was fighting over the remaining 25 percent. Crusoe was convinced that the only way for Ford Motor Company to expand its share was to take it out of B-O-P's hide. That, in turn, meant a General Motors–style assault on the medium-priced field.

When Reith returned from France, he was asked to participate on a committee headed by Crusoe to plan future company products. It is unclear how much of the plan that resulted was Crusoe and how much was Reith. Some said later that Crusoe gave Reith the assignment and let him develop it, while others pictured Reith as more of a point man for a plan Crusoe had in mind all along. In any case, Crusoe let Reith run with it, and run with it he certainly did.

The first hard evidence that something big was in the works occurred in February, 1955. The 1957 Mercury line had been approved and was slated to be, as it typically had been, a gussied-up Ford. Then, all of a sudden, an entirely new 1957 Mercury program was begun under Reith's direction. Moreover, this program called for an entirely new body shell that would be a Mercury exclusive. Larger and gaudier than any previous Mercury, it seemed to address most of the shortcomings long recognized by those in Lincoln-Mercury Division. They loved it. Crusoe and others in the Breech faction loved it, too, and it was quickly approved for production.

The flashy new Mercury was only the opening salvo in a grand strategy devised by Crusoe and Reith to put Ford Motor Company on the map in the medium-priced field. The exclusive Mercury body program was slated to be the basis for the top-end E-Car, as well, and the birth of the Edsel program can be dated from its inception.

The Crusoe-Reith plan, when it was revealed, was breathtakingly ambitious. Noting that the company had no entry at all in the upper end of the medium-priced field against Buick and Chrysler, the plan proposed adding a new brand —the E-Car—and a lot more. The specifics of the Crusoe-Reith plan were:

- Surprisingly, Mercury—not the E-Car—would be repositioned up to fill the gap between the current Mercury and the Lincoln. The E-Car would take the place of the current Mercury range, although it would involve a considerable expansion of the traditional Mercury range.

- The company would expand to three body shells: small, medium, and large. The standard Ford would be built off the small body, as would a small E-Car. The standard Mercury and a big E-Car would use the new Mercury body scheduled to be introduced for 1957. The Lincoln and a new, "Super" Mercury would be built off the big body beginning with the 1958 or 1959 model year, a body already earmarked for the next generation Lincolns. Thus, the tooling costs for each of the three bodies would be shared among two of the brands.

- The E-Car would be sold through an entirely new dealer network, including 1,200 at first and increasing to perhaps 2,500–2,600 later.
- The company would be expanded to comprise five separate automotive divisions: Ford, E-Car, Mercury, Lincoln, and Continental.

Predictably, Reith projected in his presentation that the greatest growth in the automobile market in coming years would be in the medium-priced field. With the Crusoe-Reith plan, he promised, Ford Motor Company could increase its share of industry sales from just over 30 percent to at least 35 percent by 1961. As for what all these good works would cost, it would be surprisingly modest. The mid-sized Mercury body was already in the works, so no new body shells not already in the pipeline would be required. Since the E-Car would share the Ford and Mercury bodies, it could be built right alongside those brands in their existing plants—although there would have to be some expansion of capacity. The tooling for the E-Car and the "Super" Mercury would be kept low by adopting a creative interchangeability program similar to that in use at General Motors. When Reith addressed the issue of a separate E-Car dealer network, though, he made his big pitch.

Every successful plan has a main thrust, one that ties all the elements to-

The 1957 Mercury Turnpike Cruiser on the big new Mercury body.

Edsel Division's engineering staff. *Left to right*, E. W. Reynolds, B. C. Erickson, J. W. French, B. T. Andren, and chief engineer N. L. Blume.

gether, and, for Crusoe and Reith, the compelling reason to accept the plan was the relatively small size of Ford Motor Company's current dealer body. Ford had only 8,000 dealers between Ford and Lincoln-Mercury combined. General Motors, between its five automotive divisions, had a staggering 16,500. Even Chrysler could boast of 10,000. Although Ford had regained its second place position in the industry, Chrysler, with dramatically new 1955 models, was showing signs of life and might gain back at least some of what it had lost. Ford executives also knew that taking on General Motors for first place (which was everybody's ultimate goal) would be next to impossible with half as many sales outlets as General Motors had.

Still, 8,000 dealers was impressive when you only had two franchises: Ford and Lincoln-Mercury. To go beyond that number, Crusoe and Reith contended, the company needed more franchises. The Crusoe-Reith plan called for an immediate expansion to three—Ford, E-Car, and Lincoln-Mercury-Continental—with the promise of separating Mercury and Lincoln-Continental at some point in the future. For now, simply adding the E-Car would enable the company to shoot up to 10,600 dealers, or more than Chrysler had and a big improvement over Ford's current status compared to General Motors. So, it was the dealer expansion angle that, more than any other single factor, sold the E-Car program to top management.

The Crusoe-Reith plan was formally presented to the board of directors on April 15, 1955. Henry Ford II, Breech, Crusoe, McNamara, and other top executives were in attendance. Jack Davis had just suffered a coronary and was absent. His committee, however, recommended against the plan, warning that it was too ambitious.

In particular, Davis saw trouble ahead in having Mercury abandon its customer base by moving upscale, while still offering competition for the new E-Car before the latter could become established. Davis was also concerned about tying the E-Car's fate to an untested dealer network, preferring to run it through existing dealers and then split it off later. Prior to his illness, Davis had discussed the matter with Breech and was given assurances that Breech would oppose the Crusoe-Reith plan, as well. Yet, that is not what happened. The plan was unanimously approved by the board, with Breech urging caution but going along in the end.

Breech later claimed (to anyone who would listen, it seems) that he had been the only member of the board opposed to the Edsel. That may have been true—except that he didn't oppose it when it counted. Davis, in particular, is on record as insisting that Breech had sufficient influence with Henry II to have stopped the plan if he had really wanted to do so, and there were many within the company who subsequently agreed with that assessment. According to this line of thinking, the Crusoe-Reith plan had already become embroiled in the increasingly intense politics and power plays between the product men (Breech, Crusoe, and most of the executives Breech had brought to Ford) and Whiz Kids (led by McNamara). Breech, intimidated by the growing power of the McNamara faction, and confronted with overwhelming support on the board, was reluctant to buck the tide.

However it came to pass, the decision in favor of the Crusoe-Reith plan of-

Ford Motor Company chief designer George Walker and Edsel designer
Roy Brown.

ficially launched the Edsel. A new Special Products Division was created to produce the E-Car, as it was still called, with an introduction planned for the 1957 or 1958 model year. The old Special Products Division officially became the Continental Division. (Although, confusingly, there were two different divisions with the same name within a short period of time, there was no overlap between the two.) The company thus expanded to comprise Ford, Special Products (E-Car), Mercury, Lincoln, and Continental divisions, headed by, respectively, McNamara, Richard E. Krafve, Reith, Ben D. Mills, and William Clay Ford (the youngest of the three Ford brothers). Krafve was the former assistant general manager at Lincoln-Mercury. Emmet Judge, Lincoln-Mercury's veteran product planner, was also reassigned to Special Products. Whiz Kids were now in charge of all the volume automotive divisions except, significantly, Special Products.[1]

Almost at once, Krafve and Judge set up shop in the old Henry Ford Trade School building near Ford World Headquarters in Dearborn and began organizing. Since both men had been deeply involved for several years in planning for the medium-priced field, it seemed an auspicious beginning for the

Executives seated. *Left to right*, Jack Davis, the sales vice-president; Benson Ford; Ernie Breech, the chairman; Henry Ford II, the president; Lewis Crusoe, the executive vice-president; and Walker Williams, the vice-chairman.

E-Car. A clean slate lay before them, with virtually everything about the E-Car yet to be determined—who would buy it, what it should look like, how it would be marketed and sold.

Prior to this time, George Walker had directed the styling of Ford Motor Company products as an outside consultant working through the engineering staff. In the spring of 1955, styling for all cars and trucks was officially set up as an independent department reporting to Crusoe. It was called the Styling Office and was headed by Walker, now a company vice-president. On May 12th, individual styling studios were announced for all divisions, including Special Products. The internal memo announcing the new system added:

> Each product line studio will be responsible, within the framework of Styling Office policies and practices, for all planning and development phases of production and advanced styling to meet Vehicle Division requirements. . . . Each of the Studios will obtain certain fabricating and other services on a centralized basis.[2]

In the case of the Special Products studio, it took a while to reach that advanced state, and it continued to some degree to be under the thumb of Eugene Bordinat, the head of the Mercury Studio. The original Special Products studio consisted of Roy Brown, Ken Spencer, Jim Sipple, Bob Jones, Dick Steiger, and Bert Holms. The group was headed by Brown, a Canadian still in his thirties. Brown had studied industrial design at the Detroit Art Academy and had worked as a designer for both General Motors and Ford. Spencer was placed in charge of the exterior styling, while Sipple directed the interior design.

Brown's mission was to develop "the conception of an entirely new vehicle."[3] Before any preliminary sketches had begun, many hours were spent reviewing styling both past and present, competitive and Ford Motor Company vehicles, and compiling a final list of design objectives that would give the E-Car a unique identity in the marketplace:

- To style a car with its price class having characteristics which would assure unexcelled leadership in its field.

- [To style] a completely contemporary vehicle aesthetically suggestive of top performance distinctly individual in theme and in all, capable of psychological needs of the buying public.

- Its design must also meet with the requirements of sound engineering and interchangeability.

   A. Strong product identity: Front, Side, and Rear shall be a requisite.

   B. Functional and aesthetic uniqueness shall be considered essential.[4]

In the Edsel design studio. *Standing,* Richard Krafve, Edsel Division general manager; *seated, left to right,* George Walker and William Clay Ford.

From the program's inception, one requirement was that the designers select one body shell, initially assumed to be that of the 1957 Mercury, as a basis for the E-Car design.[5] Interchangeability was, after all, at the very heart of the plan. Later, the design would be adapted to the other probable E-Car body shell, that of the Ford. The designers were also given specific limits within which they were to make their E-Car modifications. These limits restricted them to the front and rear end, bumpers, rear door lower panel, hood and deck lid. In addition, the E-Car would use its own grille, trim, and ornamentation. Krafve, a methodical man, who later estimated that four thousand individual decisions had to be made before the E-Car design saw the light of day, would describe the car as "distinctive," "immediately recognizable from the front, side, and rear," and the "epitome of the push-button era without wild-blue-yonder Buck Rogers concepts."[6] But, of course, all that was still four thousand decisions away.

During the initial planning work, Brown's group worked in a small room on the second floor of the Design Center. Previously a library, the room offered the team an opportunity to quietly develop their concepts. As ideas were tossed back and forth, the goal of giving the E-Car a unique identity became the focal point. In viewing General Motors product lines, the distinctiveness of each brand was apparent. From Chevrolet up through Cadillac, each brand had its own, well-developed design themes. This was what Brown's team had been looking for, too, a unique theme that said "E-Car."

During these early days, the team wallpapered their small studio with sketches of competitive products. One thing that stood out was that none of the cars then on the road did—i.e., stand out—at least not from the front end when viewed from any distance. Even the General Motors products used horizontal themes that tended to blend with everything else on the road from a block away. Jones, recalling the classic cars of the past and the high-grade cars then being built in Europe (Rolls-Royce, Jaguar, and Mercedes-Benz, for example), suggested using a vertical motif. Since no other American car then on the road used a vertical grille, the theme promised instant identification for the E-Car.

After the decision to use a vertical front end theme was made, Brown's team moved to the side of the car, creating the well-known "side-scallop" motif. Then, the rear-end work began with the tail lights located between the bumper and upper rear deck, much as they appeared on the 1959 model. Due to engineering and management requests, however, Brown was forced to move the tail lights up to a position at the end of the fender/deck lid line, giving the car its distinctive "gullwing" rear end theme.

Proceeding concurrently with the exterior design work, Sipple was directing work on the interior. The original concept was to have a "cockpit" approach, with the driver being the focal point for all instruments and controls, similar to what is common in the industry today. This was an early effort to use ergonomics in a car's interior design. A careful study was undertaken for the instrument panel and steering wheel. Driver comfort and ease of operation were given considerable attention. Seat contour, fabrics, and colors were also studied to reflect the basic harmony of the vehicle, and to add comfort and safety to its occupants. Brown recalled:

> We made charts on reachability. I think we were ahead of our time. But,
> we were amateurs, just starting out. Also, we were very concerned about
> safety. . . . We put the transmission push buttons in the center of the steering
> wheel. This decision was based on a study on taking the eyes off the road. It

took less time and less eye movement to punch a button in the steering wheel hub than if it was over on the left where Mercury and Chrysler put their push buttons. We made quite a study of ergonomics.[7]

In the end, the need to maintain maximum interchangeability with Ford and Mercury modified the cockpit concept to such an extent that little remained of it. About the only unique feature that survived was the the automatic transmission pushbuttons on the steering wheel hub.

Nevertheless, the design team felt they had accomplished their main goals, and they summed up the E-Car design as follows:

FUNCTIONAL AND AESTHETIC INTEGRATION

- Frontal theme combines nostalgic touch with modern straight-forward vertical thrust.
- Side-to-Rear unification creates a novel feeling of harmonious relationship and apparent increase in length from a three-quarter rear view.
- Cooling, Protection, and Dimensional requirements have been met without sacrifice of aesthetic consideration.

ROAD IDENTITY

- Strong and original frontal theme.
- Powerful design element on side elevation creating an unusual two-tone treatment.
- Trend setting rear-end theme with vigorous recognition value.[8]

While the sketch work and paper planning progressed, the library had been adequate in size. It left no room, however, for the construction of even a three-eighths-sized clay model. So, at this juncture, the studio was moved to a somewhat larger room in the Design Center basement where work on the clay models began. Two three-eighths-sized clay models were built, one an EM (Mercury-based E-car) and the other an EF (Ford-based E-Car).

As work drew to completion on the three-eighths-sized models and the rough bucks for the full-sized clay models began, space once more presented a problem. During one of his many studio visits, Crusoe remarked, "it's like trying to build a locomotive in a closet." Shortly thereafter, the studio was moved to the main floor of the Design Center.

Once the studio was moved, finishing touches were made on a fiberglass convertible. Finished in a striking turquoise-and-white color scheme, it was rushed to completion in time for presentation to the company's product planning committee.

While in its final throes, the design still underwent several last-minute changes. These included lowering the bumper pods. In early versions the pods rode higher with sheet metal lower panels, similar to the 1965 Ford Mustang. The center grille was also widened. Initially, the theme called for a much narrower center grille section than was actually built, but it was widened for engine cooling. Finally, the headlight pods were redesigned. In the early design phases, the E-Car had been tentatively scheduled for the 1957 model year. As the project moved on, however, the final release date was set for the 1958 model run when there was talk of switching over from the traditional single headlights to dual headlights. The problem was left undecided until the very end of the design process, though. This indecision required headlight pods and fenders to be wide enough to accept dual headlights and tall enough to accept the larger single headlights.

With the final decision to incorporate dual headlights, and the other minor changes completed, Brown presented the fiberglass model to the company's product planning committee in August, 1955. Even Brown did not anticipate the response the car would receive. As the curtain was opened, not a sound stirred. Then, Ernie Breech started clapping and the entire committee rose in a standing ovation. The model had been given an instant approval never before seen at the company. All those involved in the E-Car program regarded this as the best possible omen.

Sketches showing the first explorations of both hoizontal and vertical frontal themes.

Top, the second rendering with concave bumper pods. *Middle*, a third sketch that attempted to integrate the vertical and horizontal themes was rejected due to "lack of dominating center of interest"—and perhaps it looked a lot like an Olds! *Bottom*, the first rendering showing an open vertical grille similar to what appeared in production.

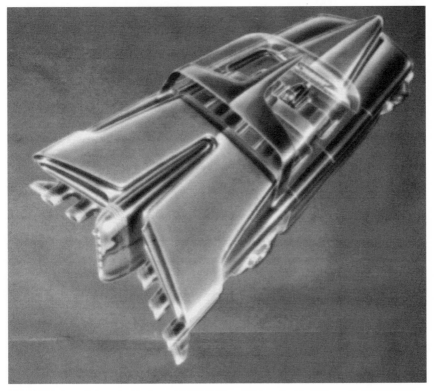

Two extremely early concept renderings. These were done nearly full size and mounted for display in the first design studio.

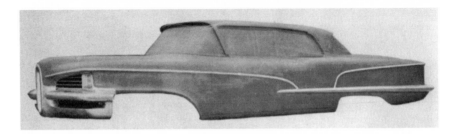

Top, an early attempt to do a two-tone concept carrying into the front and rear. *Second from top*, the first clay model using this idea. The workout of the rear fender area later led to the final scallop and rear deck integration. *Third from top*, another view of this same clay model. Note the scallops around the "C" pillar. *Right, above*, one of the many sketches in which Roy Brown and his team began to explore the gull-wing rear deck theme. *Right, below*, another sketch showing the beginnings of the rear bumper development.

Top, an early clay showing the beginnings of the vertical grille theme. *Bottom*, the grille is more refined with a center impact ring, while the shape of the hood and fender begins to take shape.

Right, above, the front
end is more refined still.
Right, below, the same clay
showing the original rear
end concept. Later, the
tail lights were moved up.
Below, most of the final
frontal design motifs ap-
pear in this clay dated
July 19, 1955, including the
grille, side grilles (with
integral parking lights),
bumpers, and the develop-
ment of the scallop treatment. Headlamps were
still single units, not
quads. This clay was also
shown to management
(probably Edsel Division,
not Ford Motor Com-
pany). *Bottom,* an earlier
clay, dated June 28, 1955,
showing development of
the gull-wing rear
treatment, but before
the side scallop had
been fully developed.

Top, another clay, dated July 19, 1955, showing the gull-wing rear and bumper treatment. *Left*, a later clay dated August 17, 1955, showing what was considered to be the approved production front end in most respects, but lacking the parking lights integrated into the grille. Instead they were worked into the bumper pods. *Below*, the other view of this clay shows a nearly final rear-end treatment.

Below, Front and rear views of the final clay as approved by management in the latter part of August, 1955. Note the quad headlamps, a last-minute change necessitated by Edsel's delayed introduction. The Edsel had originally been scheduled for a 1957 or mid-year 1957 introduction. For the 1958 model run, most American cars switched to quads.

Opposite, a series of fastback design studies: *top,* a full-size rendering; *next,* two views of a quarter-size clay model of the same idea, with revised "B" pillars on each side (it was common practice to have different treatments side-to-side on the same clay); *bottom,* yet a later Edsel clay, dated April 6, 1956.

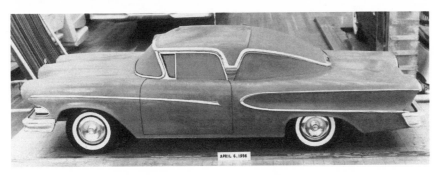

Two views of a well-developed
proposal for what became the
Citation convertible. Note the
fiberglass boot that did not make
it to production. *Top*, photo is
dated June 19, 1956, and shows
the Citation side trim in more-
or-less final form. *Bottom*, dated
May 4th, 1956, shows the side
trim in an earlier development.
Note also the tonneau cover.

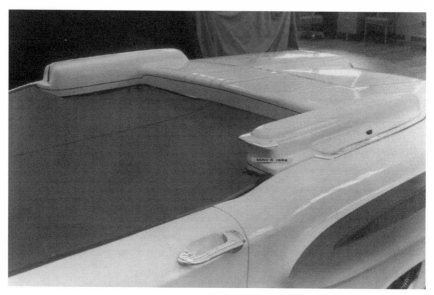

Two early rear-end treatments for
the station wagons. Both contain
elements that saw production, but
the one on the *bottom* is closer to
the actual car. Note the different
back-up lights on the bottom photo.

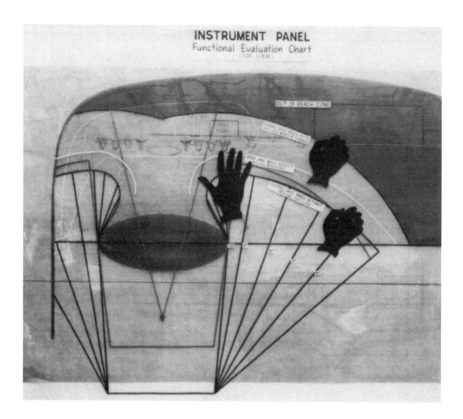

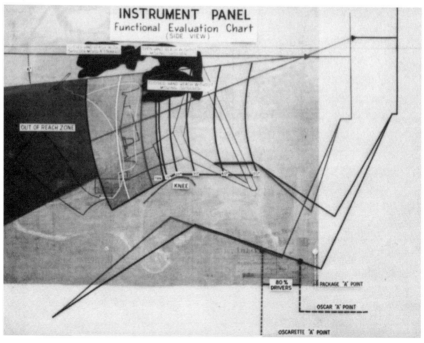

Two "functional evaluation" charts describing and illustrating the interior ergonomics the design team was studying.

SAFETY - FUNCTION

The functional pattern of this panel was established after recognizing the importance of safety considerations as a prime requisite in instrument panel design.

To incorporate safety and its functional relationship into instrument panels, the following factors must be considered:

1. DRIVER FUNCTION

Minimum driver effort is required for safe car operation. Research has determined average driver dimensions. The overlays show dimensions and instrument location.

2. BASIC DESIGN

The incorporation of soft contour treatment will insure maximum safety in impact areas.

3. GLARE

This problem is eliminated by the use of dull finish paint or textured material in glare areas.

4. REFLECTION

A cowl type cover and proper instrument location will eliminate this condition.

5. CRASH PADDING

Padding, constructed of impact tested material, applied in impact areas provides real and psychological safety.

Stages of development of the instrument panel and gauge cluster. *Directly above*, a sketch dated September 12, 1955.

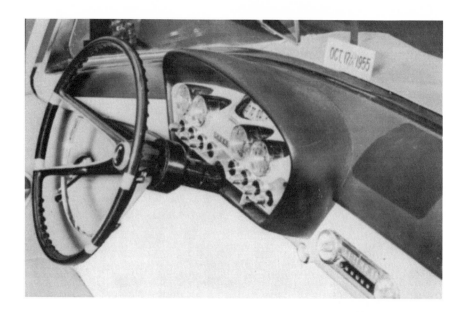

Top, a further development of instrument panel and gauge cluster, dated October 17, 1955. *Bottom*, the steering wheel and gauge cluster in more-or-less final form.

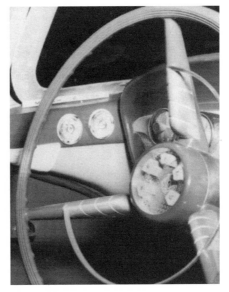

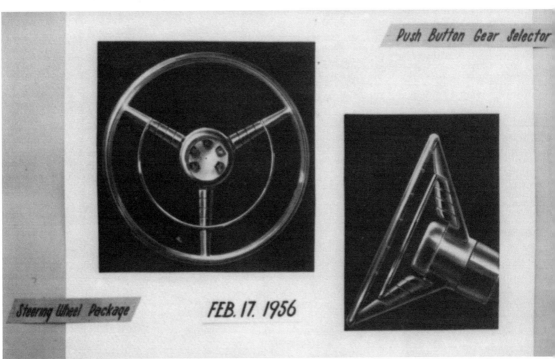

Top left, the first engineering
mock-up of the push-button
steering wheel treatment;
right, a subsequent development of the idea. *Bottom*,
renderings of the final
steering wheel design.

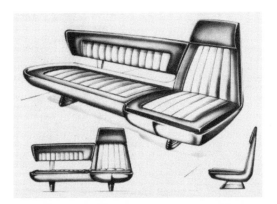

Two renderings of early seating concepts. One is stylish and contemporary, and the other, as Roy Brown notes, has "added contour and a more realistic approach to the automotive passenger requirements." *Bottom*, an early seating clay.

Opposite, final prerelease trim proposals for the Edsel model range. *Top*, Corsair. Note the non-production scallop treatment and grille insert. *Middle*, Citation. Note the absence of the inner-scallop treatment and the wide side trim molding. *Bottom*, Pacer. Note the non-standard scallop molding, the absence of side trim and the ornaments up front.

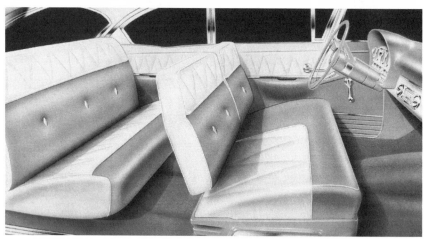

A series of final interior design proposals for various Edsel models. *Top to bottom,* Pacer sedan, Pacer two-door hardtop, and Ranger two-door hardtop.

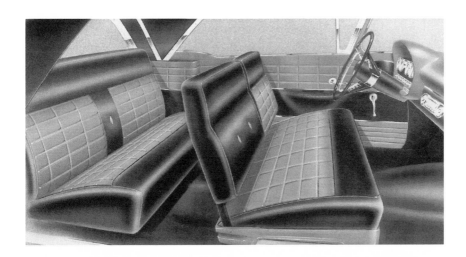

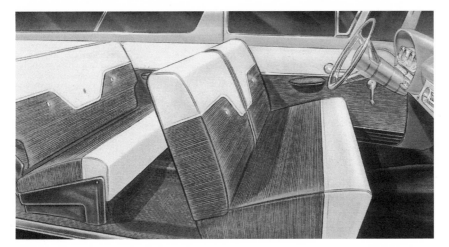

More interior design proposals. *Top to bottom*, Citation convertible, Bermuda wagon, and Roundup two-door wagon.

CHAPTER SEVEN

A Citation undergoes a water test.

Motivational Research

WITH THE ALL-IMPORTANT EXTERIOR design approved, the E-Car passed on to engineering for the production of the models to be used for preliminary engineering drawings. For the stylists, all efforts were focused on the exterior trim (hood ornaments, name scripts, series trim, etc.), as well as completion of the interior trim designs.

Meanwhile, David Wallace, a professorial-type fellow who happened to be the top product marketing specialist in the division, was hard at work analyzing the market into which the E-Car would be launched. His work would make liberal use of outside motivational research. In that, he would do nothing that would be considered the least bit out of the ordinary today. In the mid-1950s, however, it was a radical departure from the auto industry's usual way of doing business, and the Edsel's subsequent failure would set the cause of motivational research back twenty years in Detroit.

Wallace's approach to the E-Car was fairly cynical. As he related in later years:

We said to ourselves, "Let's face it, there is no great difference in basic mechanism between a $2,000 Chevrolet and a $6,000 Cadillac. Nevertheless, there's something—there's got to be something—in the makeup of a certain number of people that gives them a yen for a Cadillac, in spite of its high price—or maybe because of it.[1]

In order to figure out how to sell E-Cars, Wallace was convinced it was necessary to get down to basics and learn what prompted people to make their buying decisions. Once that was understood, the E-Car could be scientifically designed and marketed. To this end, he struck a deal with Columbia University's Bureau of Applied Social Research to help divine the answer. The university agreed to conduct in-depth interviews with 1,600 car buyers, half of them in Peoria, Illinois, half in San Bernardino, California.

Among the questions researched in this fashion were the same sort of basic ones that Emmet Judge and Dick Krafve had been discussing—without the benefit of scientific input from a prestigious university—since their Lincoln-Mercury days. What sort of images do the various automobile brands possess with the public? Who buys a Buick (or a Mercury or a Chrysler) and why? What are the identifiable segments of the buying public? What are their needs and wants in a car?

True, some of the research got a little silly, such as an analysis of the cocktail-mixing abilities of the buyers of various brands.[2] In general, though, the important questions were ones that had been asked many times before, and the answers were much the same, as well. In fact, there was little information of a substantial nature turned up in these studies that had not appeared in the plans developed, singly or together, by Judge and Krafve back at Lincoln-Mercury in 1951–52.

Early in 1956, Wallace presented his lengthy report to the division. Entitled, "The Market and Personality Objectives of the E-Car," it consisted of a good deal of socioeconomic twaddle mixed with fairly sound conclusions:

- The most advantageous personality for the E-Car might well be the smart car for the younger executive or professional family on its way up.
- Smart car: recognition by others of the owner's good style and taste.
- Younger: appealing to spirited but responsible adventurers.
- Executive or professional: millions pretend to this status, whether they can attain it or not.
- Family: not exclusively masculine; a wholesome "good" role.
- On its way up: "The E-Car has faith in you, son; we'll help you make it!"

Wallace's recommendations dovetailed nicely with Roy Brown's design goals—and it was a good thing, too, for Wallace's report was actually completed several months after the design had been approved. One wonders what

A Pacer undergoes testing at Ford's new proving ground at Romeo, Michigan.

they would have done had the two approaches ended up at divergent points. Nonetheless, the motivational research would prove useful later on when it came time to plan the launch promotion for the E-Car.

The process of naming the E-Car would be filled with both hard work and high comedy. Although many people, both in and out of the company, assumed that "E-Car" meant "Edsel," the "E" simply stood for "Experimental." (For their part, Roy Brown and his designers had referred to it as the "Ventura.") On the other hand, Krafve had actually suggested the name "Edsel" almost as soon as the project was launched. The Ford family had flatly refused the honor. Eleanor Ford, Edsel's widow, was aghast. Benson said something about naming it the Edsel over his dead body, and Henry II reportedly commented that he did not desire to see the name of his father spinning on millions of hubcaps.

So, satisfied that the name would not be Edsel, Krafve turned Wallace loose to finding another name that would be fitting. Wallace was joined in the search by Gayle Warnock, who had been named to direct Special Products Division public relations, and with other members of the Special Products Division staffs. In order to get the ball rolling in the right direction, the following list of naming parameters was devised:

1. The name shall be short, so it will display well on dealer signs.

2. It shall have two or at the most three syllables to give it cadence.

3. It should be clear and distinct to aid in radio and television identification.

4. It should start with either the letter C, S, J, F, subject to calligraphic sweep for ornaments and advertisement signatures. [Heavy foot letters as M, E, or K were to be given little consideration.]

5. It should not be prone to obscene double-entendres or jokes. Nor should it translate into anything objectionable.

6. It should be American.[3]

With these six parameters as a guide, the division began its search on two different fronts, both inside and outside the company. Internally, Wallace began testing a list of possible names, using fellow division employees as guinea pigs. Names in six-inch block letters were flashed on a screen, one by one. If one of the staff thought that the name had merit, a short pro-and-con discussion would follow. After several of these sessions the responses dwindled to nothing and the sessions were canceled. Recalled Warnock:

> It was deathly serious. We sat there motionless and soundless in the dark, staring at the screen. We were all so intense that when the name "Buick" was flashed there wasn't a murmur in the whole group.[4]

The division had better luck outside the company. It was at about this time that Foote, Cone & Belding (FC&B) was retained by the division as its advertising agency. No less a personage than Fairfax M. Cone himself would manage the account. FC&B, which had represented Hudson in years past, had beaten out dozens of agencies for the account—and was destined to regret its victory for years to come.

With what was coming to be all-too-typical overkill, Ford Motor Company had prepared a report running to several hundred pages entitled, "Procedural steps in the selection of an advertising agency for Special Products Division." Forty agencies vied for the honor. This number was eventually cut down to twenty-three. Then, eleven agencies were invited to make formal presentations. After several more rounds, the search narrowed to three agencies: FC&B, the much larger Leo Burnett agency in Chicago, and Cunningham & Wash. After weeks of waiting, FC&B was named in February, 1956.

A condition imposed upon FC&B was that the agency open and staff an office in Detroit, and one of the first assignments given to them was to assist with the faltering name search. The agency determined that one way to draw out the pent-up creativity of its people was to foster a contest within its Chicago, New York, and London offices. Nothing less than a new E-Car would be the prize for the employee who suggested the winning name. With no limit set on the individual number of entries—only the names of members of the Ford family were specifically excluded from consideration—names poured in by the thousands. Eighteen thousand, to be exact. After eliminating duplications and obvious non-starters, the agency "condensed" the list to about six thousand names. Among them were: Altair, Ariel, Arrow, Dart, Jupiter, Mars,

A Pacer in the wind tunnel.

Ovation, Phoenix, Rover, Zip, and Zoom. Phoenix reportedly had the inside track within FC&B.

At this juncture, the Lahti brothers of Ann Arbor, Michigan, who ran a marketing research company, were brought into the name game at Wallace's behest to test the names generated by FC&B. The process they chose was to send survey teams to poll people in shopping malls, train stations, bus stations, super markets, the Willow Run airport—almost any location around Ann Arbor in which willing victims might be found. Typically, the first question people were asked was something on the order of, "What do you think of when I say '————'?" This query would likely be followed with, "What word is completely opposite of '————'?" To get a representative sampling of the population, similar surveys were conducted on the East and West Coasts. As this association study progressed, it is interesting to note that four names destined to loom large in the Edsel story appeared near the top of the list (along with their word associations): Corsair (bold, romantic, devil-may-care); Citation (approving, warranting merit); and Pacer and Ranger (both associated with travel).

Still, the name search seemed a long way from success with barely a year-and-a-half to go before the launch of the E-Car. In auto industry terms, a year-and-a-half is roughly an eye-blink, so Wallace and Bob Young, also of the product planning staff, hit upon the idea of contacting someone who was, (a) skilled with words, and (b) not encumbered by familiarity with the auto industry. It so happened that Young's wife knew a poet whom she felt would

A Pacer on the skid pad.

be more than happy to assist them in their dilemma. After careful thought, and mindful of the fact that they had absolutely no authority to act on their own, a letter was drafted and sent to Marianne Moore.

As it turned out, Moore was delighted to help—if that is the right word. Her suggestions, offered in all seriousness, included such memorable examples as: Utopian Turtletop, Andante Con Moto, Mongoose Civique, Pastelogram, Intelligent Bullet, and Bullet Cloisonné. As time passed, letters continued to arrive. Name after name was submitted from the florid pen of Miss Moore, each reaching undreamed of heights of poetic fancy. Unfortunately, none of them was even remotely suitable for the E-Car.[5]

For Wallace and Young, the quality of Moore's suggestions soon became the least of their problems. While no payment had ever been offered to Moore, Christmas was approaching. Young and Wallace felt that the least they could do was send Moore some concrete expression of gratitude in keeping with the spirit of the season. Flowers would be appropriate, they thought, but since the correspondence with her had not been sanctioned, neither knew how to cover the expense. Wallace finally confided in Warnock, who graciously came to the rescue. Warnock, it seems, had a private expense account and the cost of the flowers could be buried there.

Fortunately, the Lahti brothers had had more success with the names submitted to them by FC&B. As soon as their outside research was completed, FC&B had the names all beautifully bound, tabbed, and alphabetized into six imposing volumes. The six thousand names, together with their word associations, were proudly presented to Krafve, who stared in disbelief at the mass of data in front of him and replied, "But, we don't want six thousand names. We only want one."[6]

Krafve insisted that FC&B reduce their six thousand names to no more than ten, and, what's more, gave them little more than a weekend to do it. In order to save time, both the Chicago and New York offices of FC&B were instructed to submit, independently, a list of ten names drawn from the six thousand. When the two separate lists arrived, four names appeared on both: Citation, Corsair, Pacer, and Ranger. It seems unbelievable, but it was apparently a genuine coincidence. According to Warnock, "Citation" had the inside track at this point.

So, after months of frenetic work, the expenditure of tens of thousands of dollars, with time pressing, and all other methods at a standstill, the four finalists were submitted to an executive committee meeting presided over by Breech. He looked at the finalists and said, "I don't like any of them. Let's take another look at some of the others." So, the rejects were trotted out, including Benson, Drof ("Ford" spelled backwards!), and Edsel, among others. When they got to "Edsel," Breech said, "Let's call it that."[7]

Perhaps it was no coincidence that Henry II was in Nassau, and that neither Benson nor William Clay were present at the meeting. Obviously, such a decision could not be made without their acquiescence, though, so Breech put in a long-distance call to Henry who reluctantly accepted the committee's decision, pending approval of the Ford family. The approval was eventually—

A Pacer in the "cold room." The very cold room . . .

if reluctantly—granted. The E-Car had unofficially become the Edsel. (Interestingly, the runners-up—Citation, Corsair, Pacer, and Ranger—were chosen as the series names for the line.)

There is much anecdotal evidence that the name was far from popular with many in the division. Some, like Wallace, just didn't like it on its own merits. Others thought it smacked of dynastic tendencies that would harm its public acceptance. There is no record of the response at FC&B, one of whose employees wouldn't get a free car because the rules of the game were changed after the final bell had sounded. Krafve, of course, thought Edsel was just fine, having suggested it in the first place.

Although the decision was made in the spring, the public was not let in on the secret until a few months later, on November 19, 1956. The formal announcement was as follows:

> Henry Ford II, president of Ford Motor Company, today formally announced that the company's new line of car will be named "Edsel."
>
> His announcement ended several months of public speculation concerning the car line's name. Although it had been referred to as the "E-Car" (for experimental) by engineers, and the "Ventura" by stylists, industry writers almost without exception had referred to the car as the Edsel.
>
> "I am proud and pleased to confirm that the name will be Edsel, in honor of my father who served the last twenty-four years of his life as president of Ford Motor Company," Mr. Ford said.
>
> "The new Edsel line will be introduced and marketed by a completely new dealer organization," he added.
>
> Coincidentally, Ford Motor Company's Special Products Division was renamed the Edsel Division and now is in the process of taking over offices of the Continental building at Oakwood Boulevard of the Edsel Ford Expressway in Dearborn. The move does not affect the plant area in the rear of the building, which is devoted to the assembly of the Continental Mark II. Continental Division administrative activities vacated their offices in the building when that division merged with Lincoln Division last July.
>
> The Edsel Division is headed by Mr. Richard E. Krafve, vice-president and general manager. He had been assistant general manager of the Lincoln-Mercury Division before he was given responsibility for launching the new car line.
>
> Although the division was formally organized in April of 1955, work on the new line was begun in 1948. Development was halted during the Korean conflict but studies have continued uninterrupted for the past eight years.
>
> J. Emmet Judge is manager of the product planning and merchandising offices, and responsibility for building the new dealer organization has been

given to J. C. (Larry) Doyle, a 40-year Ford veteran who is general sales and
marketing manager of the division.

Regional sales offices were established last August in five cities—Newark,
N.J., Detroit, Chicago, New Orleans and San Francisco—and twenty-four
district sales offices will be opened early next year.

Doyle announced earlier that recruitment of dealers will begin shortly
after district sales offices are opened.

Neil L. Blume, formerly executive engineer for the Lincoln-Mercury Division, is chief engineer of the Edsel Division. Roy A. Brown is chief stylist of the
Edsel under the direction of George W. Walker, vice-president [of] styling.[8]

On the day and hour of the announcement, a huge sign went up over the
building: Edsel Division. Special Products was no more. Within a short period of time, the staff employment mushroomed to 1,800 people, none of
whom, it is fair to suggest, expected that they would be out of a job in little
more than a year.[9]

CHAPTER EIGHT

The national Edsel advertising campaign included this spread
in *Life* magazine on September 9, 1957.

This is the **EDSEL**

"A remarkable new automobile joins the Ford family of fine cars"

There has never been a car like the Edsel. It is a magnificent automobile. Behind it lie all the resources of Ford Motor Company, all the experience and engineering skill.

The results are clear. The Edsel is powered by the newest V-8 engines in the world—the Edsel 400 and the Edsel 475. Their specifications: 400 and 475 pound-feet of torque; 303 and 345 horsepower; 361 and 410 cubic inches of displacement; 10.5 to 1 compression ratio. It is unlikely you have ever driven a car with so much usable power.

The Edsel's big, safe brakes do not need periodic adjustment. In the course of daily driving, they adjust automatically.

The Edsel shifts itself. In an Edsel equipped with Teletouch Drive, you just touch a button on the steering wheel hub. Teletouch Drive does the rest—smoothly, surely, safely, *electrically.*

The Edsel's list of available new features is long. Examples: contour seats; a dial that lets you select temperature, quantity and direction of air with one twist of the wrist; a warning signal that flashes when you exceed your pre-set speed limit; another that flashes when oil is one quart low; a release that enables you to open the luggage compartment from the driver's seat.

You will find there are many things that make the Edsel different from any car you have ever driven. More exciting, more sure, more safe.

What does an Edsel cost? Edsel prices range from just above the lowest to just below the highest. You can afford an Edsel. And you can choose from four series, 18 models. Your Edsel Dealer invites you to see and drive the Edsel—soon.

EDSEL DIVISION · FORD MOTOR COMPANY

EDSE

NOW AT YOUR EDSEL

As appearing in Life Magazine, September 9, 1957

The Show Opens

TO SUM UP THE PICTURE in the fall of 1956, the Edsel had been designed, researched, named, and was undergoing intensive engineering development. Running prototypes were already on the road. Dealer development and pre-launch publicity were intensifying. Meanwhile, Roy Brown and his styling team were already hard at work on the second generation models to be launched for the 1959 model year.

In the meantime, the initial Edsel advertising campaign began in the latter months of 1956 and increased in frequency and intensity as the launch date drew near in order to drive the curiosity of the general public to fever pitch. FC&B made substantial use of Wallace's motivational research, which had recommended that the Edsel be targeted toward upwardly mobile, young executive and professional families. Perhaps not wishing the Edsel to sound elitist, they changed this prescription slightly to read, "upwardly mobile, middle income, and professional families." Furthermore, Cone insisted that the word "new" be avoided as much as possible, considering the term devalued and entirely unnecessary with a car that was, obviously, entirely new anyway. Curiously, he also sought to contain the creative impulses of his people in preparing the ad campaign. He explained his strategy to the press:

We think it would be awful for the advertising to compete with the car. We hope no one will ever ask, "Say, did you see that Edsel ad?" in any newspaper, magazine, or on television, but, instead, that hundreds of thousands of people will say, and say again, "Man, did you read about that Edsel?" or "Did you see that car?" This is the difference between advertising and selling.[1]

One is left wondering what, exactly, he meant. Did he really believe that the purpose of advertising isn't to sell the product? How could advertising be so low-key that people didn't remember it . . . and still have them remember the product being advertised?

No matter. Fairfax Cone wasn't the only man associated with the Edsel to get wrapped up in his own brilliant conception. Everyone connected with the program seems to have been similarly infected to some degree. It was almost a mob psychosis with everyone on an Edsel high.

Prospective dealers were certainly on a high. One of the real tragedies of the Edsel—due to its ultimate consequences for those directly involved—was the success J. C. "Larry" Doyle, Edsel Division's general sales and marketing manager, had in signing up a new dealer network. The initial goal was to have the first 1,200 Edsel dealers in place from coast-to-coast by "E-Day"—finally pegged for September 4, 1957.

Krafve insisted that they go after the best quality dealers in every community, even if it meant stealing dealers away from other brands, even if it meant pitching Ford and Lincoln-Mercury dealers (although Ford and Lincoln-Mercury dealers would be allowed to keep their existing franchises). Krafve's concern was understandable not only because he naturally wanted high-quality outlets, but also in the context of 1956. Dealers and their sharp practices had been the subject of state and national investigations in the several years leading up to the launch of the Edsel. High-pressure tactics, price-fixing, and other deplorable doings were very much on the consumer's mind. Worse, the auto companies were fingered as colluding—directly or indirectly—in many of these practices. During Congressional hearings, no less a figure than Alfred Sloan was personally mortified to discover what his automotive divisions were doing to General Motors' dealers and, in turn, forcing the dealers to do to their customers. Sloan, by all accounts, really hadn't known what had been going on. By the time the Edsel dealer program was set in motion, Krafve certainly did and he was determined to maintain a high standard. He explained his position in simple terms:

A customer who gets poor service on an established brand blames the dealer. On an Edsel, he will blame the car.[2]

Larry Doyle.

It wasn't for nothing that Larry Doyle had spent forty years selling cars at Ford Motor Company. Few men knew the sales end of the business better than he did, and he set about his dealer development assignment with gusto. He knew that in order to attract the type of dealers Krafve wanted—who, in many cases, were being asked to give up profitable franchises with Ford's competitors—he would have to have the right approach. As soon as a few prototypes were available, he sent them around to Edsel Division's regional offices. There, kept under lock and key, each car awaited prospective dealers. The car was the bait. Every dealer for miles around would want to get a look at it, Doyle knew, if only out of curiosity. So, Doyle would send his men into a given territory, determine the top couple of dealers in each community, and offer to show them an Edsel—if they were serious about discussing an Edsel franchise, and willing to prove it by sitting through an hour-long presentation. It worked like a charm. In fact, many dealers were ready to sign up as soon as they saw the car. By the summer of 1957 Doyle was close to his initial goal of having 1,200 first-rate dealers by E-Day.

Doyle, whether he realized it or not, did more than create a dealer network. He committed the Edsel program. As Krafve noted years later, the plug could have been pulled on the Edsel at any point until the company had incurred obligations to all those dealers. Once that had been done, there was no alternative but to build Edsels.

In June, 1957, it was announced that Ford Motor Company had set aside

$250 million for the Edsel launch. Of this, $150 million had been spent to up-grade Ford and Mercury plants and facilities where the Edsel would be built, $50 million had been spent on Edsel tooling, and the final $50 million was earmarked for initial advertising and promotion. This was described by business publications (and not denied by Ford Motor Company) as being the most money ever spent launching a consumer product.

Also in June, the first Edsel television commercials were filmed. An Edsel was shipped under tight security to Hollywood where Cascade Pictures did the filming. This was the same company that produced hush-hush flicks for the Atomic Energy Commission. The actors and actresses employed had to swear that they wouldn't blab a syllable about the new car until E-Day.

On July 15th, the first actual Edsels moved majestically down final assembly lines in four plants around the country: Sommerville (Massachusetts), Mahwah (New Jersey), Louisville (Kentucky), and San Jose (California). Then, on July 22nd, the first regular magazine advertisement from FC&B appeared in Life magazine. A "teaser" ad done in glorious black-and-white, it showed a blurred Edsel roaring down a highway. "Lately, some mysterious automobiles have been seen on the roads," the headline read. This ad was followed by another two weeks later, which illustrated an Edsel under a car cover at the entrance to the Ford Design Center. It was headlined (referring to the new Edsel dealers), "A man in your town recently made a decision that will change his life." A truer advertisement was never published.[3]

At this juncture, virtually everything that could be done had been done. The car was designed, engineered, tested, and in production. The marketing and advertising campaigns had been completed. The dealers has been signed up and were preparing to open. The Edsel Division was fully staffed and humming with activity. About the only thing left was the launch itself. The responsibility for seeing that it went off with the proper amount of enthusiasm fell to Gayle Warnock, the newly appointed public relations director.

Warnock's job was not so much to drum up interest in the Edsel—for there could hardly have been more of that by the spring of 1957—but to channel it in the right directions and see that it stayed at fever pitch until E-Day. Warnock had hardly been biding his time heretofore. The interest, indeed enthusiasm, Doyle had found in prospective dealers was partly due to Warnock's early public relations efforts. Warnock was now, however, to out-do himself.

Warnock, a small, stylish man with a thin mustache, had been brought from the Chicago Ford Division office by Krafve. Krafve had realized from the first that the problem with Edsel publicity would be to "program" it. In other words, generating interest would not be the problem; the problem would be

Emmet Judge.

in orchestrating the interest that was already building when Warnock came on board. Warnock, who had spent his life at the company trying to invent creative ways to drum up publicity—a role at which he was, by all accounts, extremely adept—was faced with the easiest public relations "challenge" of his career. Everyone, it seemed, wanted to know all about the new Edsel. Indeed, it soon became clear to him that the real challenge was in not over-selling it.

"When they find out it's got four wheels and one engine, just like the next car," Warnock warned Krafve one day, "they're liable to be disappointed."[4] Warnock's solution to this quandary, was to undertake what the *New York Times* later referred to as the "strip tease" approach, i.e., to reveal a little about it at a time. Krafve, Doyle, and Judge were sent on speaking tours around the country as 1957 wore on. Krafve tried to play it low key, but Judge—he of the celebrated "paper doll show" in 1951 that arguably started the Edsel on its way—developed a multi-media spectacular that cost $5,000 each time he presented it. And, he presented it often, from coast-to-coast, with unbridled enthusiasm for the forthcoming Edsel. True, he didn't show much of the actual car, but audiences were so spellbound by his pyrotechnics and infectious excitement that they forgot to notice.[5]

It was hard to keep the story a secret. Part of Warnock's problem was that the launch had originally been scheduled for June. Later, this was pushed back to September so as to keep the Edsel from stealing sales from Ford and Mercury during the end-of-model-year summer clean-up months. But, as a result,

The E-car incognito.

the story was increasingly difficult to keep under wraps. In its February, 1957, issue, *Motor Trend* published a report that included astonishingly accurate drawings of the Edsel. The magazine called them "speculations," but, clearly, someone who knew what the Edsel looked like had tipped them off. Whether this was a deliberate "leak" by Ford Motor Company—which is entirely possible— or something more subterranean cannot be determined at this juncture.

By the summer of 1957, however, the news was spreading quickly and Warnock was being besieged by automotive writers wanting a look at the car. He obliged a few favored journalists with quick "you've-seen-it-now-forget-it" one-on-one previews, but the cover was blown for good in August when the *Saturday Evening Post* published a feature article—complete with photos— telling everything. That took a lot of the edge off Warnock's carefully planned national press preview scheduled a few days later.

The formal press preview was the three-day affair that began on August 26th. Warnock had proposed staging the preview either on a steamboat in the Detroit River ("wrong symbolism"), or in Edsel, Kentucky ("inaccessible by road"), or in Haiti ("just turned down flat").[6] All of these ideas were rejected in turn. So, two hundred and fifty auto writers were invited from all across the country to hear the formal presentations and drive the Edsel in Dearborn. To make sure it would be special, he invited the journalists to bring their wives along, which was an unusual practice.

On the first full day of the preview, Henry II offered a few words, and the formal presentations were made. The following day, August 27th, the journalists were treated to an exciting stunt driving exhibition at the Ford Proving

Ground and allowed to drive the cars themselves. That evening, the guests were invited to a mock night club fashioned for the event in the Design Center. The next morning, Ernie Breech personally gave the journalists and their wives a send-off, proclaiming, "It's a husky youngster, and, like most other new parents, we're proud enough to pop our buttons."[7] Then, seventy-one of the journalists were presented with new Edsels to drive home and personally deliver to dealers in their communities. The tab for the entire affair was $90,000—an enormous sum for a press presentation in those days.

It all went pretty well, although not entirely without hitches. The only hotel Warnock could arrange was the unfortunately named Sheraton-Cadillac in Detroit. The celebrated Ray McKinley band, which had been retained for the night club gala at the Design Center, still used music stands held over from when it had been the Glenn Miller band. They were all emblazoned with the letters "GM." Finally, several of the new Edsels failed to reach their destinations. One journalist wrecked his. Another had the oil pan fall out of his car and the engine freeze up. Another got the scare of his life when his car smashed through a turnpike tollgate due to faulty brakes. Still another was sideswiped on the Pennsylvania Turnpike by a driver so eager to get a look he got too close.

Then, barely a week later, on September 3rd, prices were formally announced. They covered virtually the entire spectrum of the medium-priced field, from $2,519 to $3,801. The following day, September 4th, was E-Day.

"A man in your town recently made a decision that will change his life."

Before the day was over, it was estimated that 2,850,000 people had trooped down to their local Edsel dealers to see the new car.

What America saw on that Wednesday was a new brand of automobile offered in four lines with eighteen body styles, and three station wagon lines with five body styles. The single feature of the Edsel that caught the public's fancy most forcefully was, as expected, the vertical grille. The reaction fell into two camps, favorable and unfavorable. The grille was quickly dubbed the "horse collar" grille by many. Others, less complimentary, said it looked like a toilet seat or, worse, like a part of the female anatomy. Within the industry, it was described as looking like "an Oldsmobile sucking a lemon." No one could deny, however, that the Edsel design had made a dramatic impact.

Leading the line-up were the Citation and Corsair lines, based on the Mercury body shell and built on the Mercury assembly lines. The standard (and only) power team for the Citation and Corsair was the all-new E-475 V8 mated with Teletouch drive automatic transmission with the push buttons on the steering wheel hub.

The Citation—the top of the line—was offered in two- and four-door hardtop styles, and a two-door convertible. The convertible featured a newly designed wraparound rear window. The slightly less expensive Corsair was available in two- and four-door hardtop body styles. Items standard on the Citation and Corsair, and optional for the rest of the Edsel line, included luxurious trim accessories such as carpets, foam rubber seat cushions, and interior courtesy lights. The price of all this luxury and style ranged from $3,346 for the Corsair two-door hardtop to $3,801 for the Citation convertible.

The E-475 engine was based on the Lincoln-Mercury 430-cubic-inch V8, using the same stroke with a smaller bore to give it a reduced displacement of 410 cubic inches. In that form, the engine was unique to the Edsel. It was also unique in that it had a new, three-stage dual-thermostat cooling system. After starting and during warm-up, water circulation was restricted to the heads and intake manifold. As water temperature increased to a level of 140 degrees, the water was circulated through the block until the engine reached its final operating temperature of 180 degrees, causing the second thermostat to open and water to then circulate through the entire cooling system. This system, although presenting maintenance problems later, offered faster engine warm-up, increased fuel economy, and longer engine life.

The Teletouch drive transmission was a three-speed automatic with, as noted previously, the control buttons ingeniously located in the center of the steering wheel hub. With just the touch of a button, the transmission could be shifted between park, reverse, drive, or low range. Designed for luxury and ease of

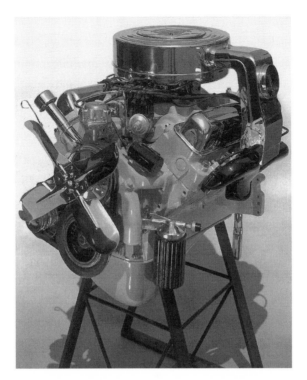

Corsair-Citation 410 cubic inch V8 engine.

driver operation, this transmission nevertheless caused a multitude of service problems and was discontinued at the end of the 1958 model year.

The Ford-based Pacer and Ranger lines were designed for people who liked the Edsel, but wanted a more affordable package. The standard power team was the E-400 V8, which displaced 361 cubic inches, and manual shift, three-speed transmission. The E-400 was a big brother to the Ford 332 and 352 cubic inch V8 engines, and a near twin to the Ford 361 cubic inch Police option. All four were totally new in design when introduced in 1958.

The Pacer was offered in two- and four-door hardtop, four-door sedan, and two-door convertible body styles. The least expensive Edsel, the Ranger, came in two- and four-door hardtop, and two- and four-door sedan versions. The prices ranged from a modest $2,519 for the Ranger two-door sedan to $3,028 for the sporty Pacer convertible.

But, that was not all. For the families who demanded the room that only a station wagon could provide, the line-up offered no less than five different station wagons in three different series. All station wagons, regardless of trim level, were based on the Ford station wagon body.

The most luxurious of the wagons was the four-door Bermuda, in six- or nine-passenger versions. The Bermuda carried the elegance of woodgrain side trim and two-tone paint and a $3,190 price tag. Somewhat plainer, due to the absence of the wood-grain, was the four-door Villager, also available in six- or nine-passenger versions. With both the Bermuda and the Villager, a third seat was added to the vehicle to convert the six-passenger version to the nine-passenger version. The most unique Edsel station wagon offering was the low-priced two-door Roundup. It came only in six-passenger-form and listed for $2,876.

The standard power team for the wagon series was the same as that offered in the Pacer and Ranger lines—the E-400 V8 and three-speed manual transmission. Power team options limited to the Pacer, Ranger, and station wagon lines included overdrive for the three-speed manual, and, of course, the Edsel Teletouch automatic.

All Edsel models came standard with a host of unique features, large and small: the new self-adjusting brakes, the wraparound front turn signals, the safety cone steering wheel, and the aircraft-type control center instrument panel with its unique floating compass-like speedometer. To further "personalize " any 1958 Edsel, a long list of optional equipment was offered, including such common items as power steering, power windows, power door locks, power brakes, and power seats. New accessories designed specifically for the Edsel included the 'Dial-Temp' air system, where, with one knob, ventilation, heating, or air-conditioning (also an option) could be set to a desired comfort level. Safety options included a speed warning light that would cause the speedometer to turn red when exceeding a speed pre-set by the driver. Also available was Touch-Lubrication (Citation and Corsair only) that allowed the driver to lube the chassis with the touch of a control knob on the dash. The extensive accessory list also offered such items as a panel-mounted compass, a tachometer, a remote trunk release, a power antenna, a radio, and safety warning lights.

Even the two-tone exterior paint combinations were unique to the Edsel. Any one of eighteen solid exterior colors could be specified, but there were also scallop two-tone and scallop-and-roof two-tone treatments. In the former, the area within the rear scallop, including the rear panel below the tail lights, was of a pleasing and contrasting color, while, in the scallop-and-roof version, the roof was also painted the same color as the scallop.

In all, the new Edsel line-up was impressive for its wide range of models and its extensive list of features and accessories. Little effort, it seemed, had been spared to give Edsel dealers the hardware they needed to appeal to the widest possible range of prospects. All that remained was to see how those prospects would respond.

Years later, employees of FC&B were still talking about the big party thrown in Dearborn at the time of the introduction. Everyone who was anyone was there, including all the important big-wigs from Ford Motor Company. As the story goes, at one point in the evening McNamara walked up to Fairfax Cone and commented matter-of-factly:

> Of course, you realize you're going to have to let all of these people go. We've decided to discontinue the Edsel.[8]

Top, a 1958 Citation convertible; *bottom*, a Villager station wagon.

A Bermuda station wagon.

A Pacer two-door hardtop with the optional tri-tone paint scheme.

A Pacer convertible with the optional back-up lights.

A Ranger two-door sedan.

A Corsair four-door hardtop.

A Roundup wagon.

A Pacer four-door hardtop with optional front bumperguards.

A Citation two-door hardtop.

A Ranger four-door sedan.

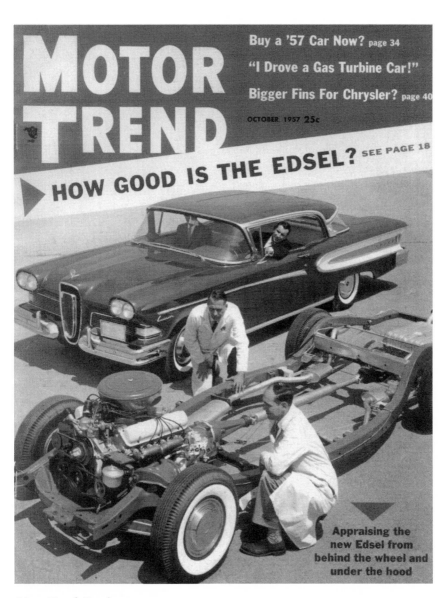

Motor Trend, October, 1957.

CHAPTER NINE

1959 Ford Thunderbird.

First Tragedy . . .

LOOKING BACK, it was in the early months of 1956 that the grand strategy developed by Lewis Crusoe and Jack Reith—of which the Edsel was the most visible component—began to unravel. It started, innocently enough, with a decision to build a four-passenger Thunderbird for the 1958 model year.

The story of the 1958-series Thunderbirds—the so-called "Square 'Birds"—began in January, 1955, when Robert McNamara was named to head Ford Division. The 1958 model already in development was a restyled version of the 1955–57 two-seater. Styling photos show a car very similar to the 1957 model, but with a rear-end treatment that looked very much like what eventually appeared in 1958.

Since McNamara was the quintessential bean counter, one of the first things he did was to reexamine Ford's product line with an idea to weeding out the slow-selling models. The way he saw it, there was simply no sense in building anything unless you built a lot of them and the two-seater Thunderbird wasn't making the grade. The key to McNamara's vision for increasing the Thunderbird's appeal was enlarging the car substantially, adding a rear seat, and making it a true four-passenger conveyance. Initially, he insisted that a station wagon model be considered, too.

Yet, there was serious debate within the company as to whether even the hardtop could be justified. One internal report suggested it would lose as much as $7 million over its projected three-year life span. What may have saved it was the decision by Earle MacPherson, the company's chief engineer, to build it with unibody (frameless) construction. This would be a first for Ford and, it was hoped, would bolster the company's middling image as a technology leader. Unibody was thought within the industry to be the wave of the future, and the idea of gaining experience with a relatively low-volume line such as the Thunderbird was quite attractive to company executives—and especially to McNamara.

The problem this posed was that projected Thunderbird volume, even in four-seater form, would not justify the entirely new facility being planned at Wixom, Michigan, to produce it. MacPherson's answer to that was to order Lincoln Division to switch its cars to Wixom, as well. Since it was impossible to build both unibody and body-and-frame cars on the same assembly line, Lincoln would have to switch to unibody.[1]

Lincoln Division was immediately thrown into an uproar. Harley Copp, Lincoln's chief engineer, insisted that (a) there wasn't time to do an entirely new Lincoln for 1958, (b) there certainly wasn't enough time to do it with a new (to Ford) technology never before attempted for a car of the Lincoln's size, and (c), even if it worked, unibody technology made annual styling changes far more difficult and expensive. This last point was critical in the luxury segment where being able to respond quickly to market demands was essential. Copp was correct; the 1958 Lincoln proved to be a disaster for all the reasons noted.[2]

With Lincoln going unibody, the Crusoe-Reith plan was suddenly approaching something akin to shambles. Lincoln Division was back where it had started, having to foot the bill for its own body—i.e., exactly the ruinously wasteful practice the Lincoln-Mercury, Davis, Judge-Krafve, and Crusoe-Reith plans had sought to end. Worse, there was no longer a Lincoln body to share with the "Super" Mercury, and that all-important product would have to be downgraded to the mid-size body. That, in turn, made it far more difficult to move Mercury sufficiently upscale to keep it from colliding with the projected E-Car. In addition, with the standard Mercury, the Super Mercury, and the big E-Car all sharing the same body and general specifications, it would be that much harder to position any of them successfully. This problem would be especially acute for the E-Car, which was heavily dependent upon assuming much of the traditional Mercury customer base. If Mercury wasn't moving upscale—or wasn't moving up enough to open a meaningful gap between Ford and Mercury—who would buy the E-Car? Still, at the time, the big losers seemed to be Mercury and Lincoln.

Then, in the summer of 1956, Crusoe suffered a heart attack. Although he was expected to continue on as executive vice-president with responsibility for the car and truck divisions, his ability to monitor their activities waned sharply. In particular, Reith no longer had an aggressive patron at the highest levels of the company, nor did the grand strategy for expansion into the medium-priced field that he and Crusoe had devised.

A further storm warning came in November, 1956, with the hiring of James J. Nance. Nance had been president of Packard since 1952, and of Studebaker-Packard since the latter's takeover of the former in the fall of 1954. By the summer of 1956, Studebaker-Packard was on the rocks, although Nance's reputation as a manager and marketing expert was still intact. The decline of Studebaker-Packard, although not an appropriate subject for this book, was caused largely by factors beyond Nance's control.[3]

In early 1956, Nance had attempted to arrange a takeover of Studebaker-Packard by Ford. The offer was declined, but, in the wake of Crusoe's sudden deterioration in health, Breech sought out Nance as a trusted ally in his growing power struggle with McNamara and the Whiz Kids. Thus, Nance was named vice-president of marketing, a move which enraged McNamara and his faction. They felt they had been patient enough in waiting for Breech and Crusoe to retire within the next several years. Nance, however, was ten years younger than either and bore all the earmarks of an heir-apparent. Unknown to Breech and Nance, the Whiz Kids secretly met and began plotting strategy.[4]

In May, 1957, Crusoe was finally forced by ill health to retire as executive vice-president and McNamara took his place. That meant that the quintessential bean counter—a man who, by all accounts, had little knowledge about cars and even less love for them—was now calling the shots for all of Ford Motor Company's car and truck divisions. Moreover, McNamara was a man who had no particular affection for Edsel Division's general manager, Krafve, who, alone among the divisional heads at this point, was not a Whiz Kid. McNamara had even less affection for Nance, the only man who still stood between him and virtual day-to-day control of Ford Motor Company. As long as Nance survived—with his pipeline to Breech in the chairman's office, and his authority for overall corporate marketing and product planning—McNamara and the Whiz Kids were forced to bide their time.

Insofar as the Edsel was directly concerned, the numbers that McNamara worshipped were rapidly turning against it. To be sure, there were more than a few in the company who were having second thoughts. Mostly, this was be-

From left to right, Robert S. McNamara, group vice-president; James O. Wright, general manager, Ford Division; and Charles R. Beacham, assistant general manager, Ford Division.

cause the medium-priced field was in trouble. In the two years since the E-Car had been conceived, there had been nearly a 40 percent decline in the numbers of automobiles sold in that segment, a decline that far outpaced the 16 percent decline in new car sales overall.

Then, in June, 1957, the stock market took a nose dive. Although no one realized it at the time, it was the beginning of the 1958 recession. By August, sales of medium-priced cars—which had hardly been robust in 1956 and 1957

—took another dip. As the 1957 model year came to a close in the late summer of 1957, dealers for all brands had more unsold cars on hand than at any time in recent memory.

Reith's 1957 "Big M" Mercury line—minus the Super Mercury, which was not scheduled until 1959—was doing somewhat better than the medium-priced field as a whole; it was down only 30 percent. Still, by the summer of 1957, there were rumors around the company that Reith was in trouble. He was giving too much attention to the product, it was said, and not enough managing Mercury Division. It is likely, however, that the rumors also had to do with corporate politics.[5] One wonders if it is coincidental that such rumors should have gained currency simultaneously with the rise of McNamara. Richard Stout, a product planner at Lincoln-Mercury and at Edsel in the 1950s, contends, however, that Breech was after Reith in part because of growing anger over the problems developing with the Crusoe-Reith plan:

> Breech went after him because his plan was a failure and because of the condition of Mercury Division. Quality control was very bad. Then, Breech said that Reith was lying to him about the quality of the cars. But, I think that a lot of the thing had to do with the Edsel project that he had brought them into.[6]

As for the Edsel, the story circulated in subsequent years at Foote, Cone & Belding regarding McNamara's statement that it was being discontinued before it had officially gone on sale (see the end of Chapter Eight) seems difficult to believe without corroboration. FC&B was not the only source, however. Stout, who worked directly with Nance during this period, tells a similar story about the company party just prior to the launch of the Edsel:

> In the evening, a dinner dance was held at the elaborately transformed Styling Rotunda. Top company officials and spouses, including the [Ford] brothers and their wives, the Breeches, the Nances, officials of Edsel Division, and their wives, were there as were other honored guests. Robert S. McNamara, of course, was in attendance. . . . Happy, smiling faces exchanged congratulations—compliments and words of goodwill were heard all around—relaxation and joy prevailed after years of looking forward to the great day. . . . Word got to Nance that McNamara had made a remark about "phasing out" the car that had not even been introduced yet.[7]

The two versions of the story come from entirely different sources and agree on so many points that it is difficult to dismiss. Of course, even McNamara did not yet possess the clout to kill the Edsel outright. Nance still stood in his way. On the other hand, McNamara was a proven master at killing things through devious means—Jim Nance being high on the hit list.

Left to right, Henry Ford II and Ernie Breech.

The day after E-Day, on September 5th, it was announced that Nance was being reassigned to head a consolidated Lincoln and Mercury Division—which would include Mercury, Lincoln, and Continental nameplates—and McNamara was taking over corporate marketing and product planning.[8] The corporation was now reduced to three divisions: Ford, Edsel, and Lincoln and Mercury. The consolidation achieved two things: 1) it saved Ford Motor Company around $80 million a year in overhead, and 2) it put Nance below the corporate vice-president responsible for the car and truck divisions on the organization chart. Nance was now reporting to McNamara.

The only thing that could save the Edsel now was a stellar sales perform-ance. Even McNamara wouldn't kill a car that was selling up a storm. On E-Day, more than 6,500 Edsels were either delivered to eager customers or or-dered for future delivery. It seemed a promising start. In the first ten days of September—during only six of which the Edsel was officially on sale—4,095 were actually sold. By the end of the month, however, the ten day sales rate had declined to around 3,600; and, in the first ten-day reporting period in October, it took a disheartening dip to only 2,751. This was an annual sales rate of around 100,000 cars per year—half what the company had projected and felt it needed to defray its investment. On October 13th, the enormously popular Ed Sullivan Show was pre-empted for an Edsel spectacular starring Bing Crosby and Frank Sinatra. The reported cost was $400,000, but it, too, failed to light a fire under the smoldering Edsel.

Surprisingly, considering the above, early sales were quite strong in some regions of the country. In Wayne County, Michigan—the county that com-prised most of the Detroit Metropolitan area, and which was often used as a barometer for car sales within the industry—the Edsel sold very well, hitting 3.5 percent of new car sales in September. Dealers in the Southwest also did well. A number of the large, metropolitan dealers in the East reported run-ning ahead of their quotas and even had trouble getting enough cars. This re-inforced suspicions that at least part of the problem was the relative weakness of many of the new dealers.

Even some of those Edsel dealers whose initial sales were strong, however, were manifestly displeased with the way the launch had been orchestrated by the company. The complaints were numerous. W. T. Wilson, a Detroit Edsel dealer, complained:

> The Edsel was introduced so far ahead of the new models of other cars that it
> hindered sales instead of helping them. Customers waited to see the other
> cars before buying.[9]

Another Edsel dealer, voicing a related complaint, took aim at the launch advertising, which had not referred to the new Edsel as a 1958 car. That, com-bined with the early introduction, apparently confused some car buyers. Said the dealer:

> It was just plain stupid. None of the advertising ever mentioned the fact that
> the car was a 1958 model. People came into my showroom by the hundreds,
> and half of them wanted to know if this was the 1957 Edsel or the 1958 Edsel.
> Some of them said that the '57 Edsel I had on the floor wasn't bad, but they'd
> wait until the '58 Edsel came out. When my salesmen would try to explain

Left to right, James Nance and Ben Mills.

that this was the 1958 Edsel, the customers thought we were trying to pull a fast one. They walked out [of the show-room].[10]

In response to similar complaints, national advertising was quickly modified to specify that this was, indeed, the 1958 Edsel. By then, of course, all the other 1958 cars were out and the damage had been done. Dealers also complained about getting early cars that were loaded with options and, therefore, far more expensive than prospects expected. Other dealers reported being overloaded with the pricier Corsair and Citation models, and bereft of the more affordable

Rangers and Pacers that people wanted to buy. This form of self-inflicted "sticker shock" is a frequent problem with new models from any manufacturer, but it hardly helped the cause.

Part of the problem, to be sure, was that the 1958 Edsels bore higher 1958 price tags. Initially, all the other cars on the market were 1957 models that not only bore lower prices, on average, but were subject to year-end discounts besides. Mercury Division was part of the problem, too. Sales of Reith's new "Big M" Mercurys softened drastically as the summer wore on and the division was forced to undertake an emergency, thirty-day advertising campaign to cut prices and clear out 1957 model inventories. All of this was beginning to take a toll on Edsel dealers. Charles Kreisler, a long-time Manhattan Olds dealer who had been one of Larry Doyle's most conspicuous converts, announced at the end of November that he was dropping his Edsel franchise and switching to Rambler instead.

After the fact, in their personal postmortems, Edsel Division executives were widely divergent in recalling when they decided the Edsel was in trouble. Warnock claimed to have sensed it as early as a couple of weeks after E-Day. Krafve got cold feet toward the end of October, while Doyle held out until mid-November. Wallace insisted years later that the turning point was October 4th—the day the Soviet Sputnik space craft went into orbit, and Americans suddenly began to question the validity of the American Dream itself.

The date of September 5th—the day of McNamara's accession—stands out, though. It would be unfair to say he hated the Edsel per se, for it went deeper than that. He hated complexity his bean-counter mind couldn't understand. Later, as Secretary of Defense in the 1960s, he would achieve notoriety for his insistence that the Air Force and Navy share a common jet fighter. The resulting F-111—known derisively as the "Flying Edsel"—was a compromise aircraft that did nothing especially well, but he simply could not see why the Pentagon wanted to spend all that money to develop two or three jet fighters that all looked pretty much the same to him. So it was with cars.

Since 1953, the trend at Ford Motor Company had been toward expansion and complexity. Body shells had proliferated as well as entire divisions. In 1946, there had been two automotive body shells and one division. By the end of 1956, the number of body shells had grown to five, as had the number of independent car divisions.[11] After McNamara was named executive vice-president in May, 1957, the trend was quickly reversed. Continental Division was the first to go, and, within a few short months, Lincoln and Mercury were consolidated —and it wouldn't stop there.

Then, in December, 1957, a "1960–1961 New Car Interchangeability Program" was issued over McNamara's signature. It called for Ford, Edsel, and Mercury products (excluding the Thunderbird) to share a single common body shell by 1961 when the next new Ford body was scheduled. The budget for the 1961 Edsel was put at a modest $30 million for "unique exterior panels"—i.e., sheet metal. Except for unique trim and upholstery, everything else would be Ford. The Mercury program—budgeted at a more respectable $62 million— called for a product line "generally similar to Edsel, but with additional unique parts for extended 'Park Lane' series, and more unique chassis items."[12] The Park Lane series on a stretched Ford body was all that would be left of Jack Reith's ambitious Super Mercury. It was a dramatic comedown for the Edsel, too, and it was hard to see how they were going to do much with $30 million and a Ford body, but it is worth noting that a 1961 Edsel program was still an active part of corporate planning at this point.

Meanwhile there was the faltering 1958 line to think about. In December, 1957, Henry Ford II was forced to go on a nationwide television hook-up to reassure nervous Edsel dealers that "the Edsel is here to stay."[13] Emmet Judge followed with one of his by-then-patented extravaganzas comparing the new Edsel to the competition from General Motors and Chrysler. Around the same time, the division sent a million-and-a-half letters to medium-price class prospects inviting them to drop by their local Edsel dealer, take a test drive, and get a scale model Edsel as a gift. The division picked up the tab for the entire promotion, including the model cars, and began offering dealers "bonuses" of up to $300 on each car sold. Edsel advertising also began to sound a bit frantic, with claims of the car's "success" repeated again and again, as if saying the word would make it happen.

As if to prove that there wasn't going to be much help from any quarter, though, early press reports were decidedly tepid. The influential segment of the press that routinely covered the auto industry was underwhelmed. *Motor Trend* featured the Edsel on the cover of its October, 1957, issue in what was probably the most important "expert" opinion circulated among the general public. The eight-page feature was entitled, "How good is the Edsel?" The answer was mixed. Concluded *Motor Trend*:

> Definitely a cut apart from the majority of cars, it is extremely doubtful whether there will be a style remotely like the Edsel, at least in most components, within the next twelve months. However, lest we be accused of unduly "raving" about it, let us say this: Edsel has . . . several unique approaches . . . but there were untold opportunities for more. To some all the subtly increased fanfare over the past two years may seem to have been unwarranted—to others who can appreciate a fresh approach to styling

and desire distinction unobtainable in Ford, Chevrolet, or Plymouth, the Edsel may well be the answer.[14]

In its December issue, *Motor Trend* featured a cross-country road test of both Pacer and Corsair models. The former had been meticulously prepped by factory mechanics prior to being handed over to *Motor Trend*, the latter, significantly, had not. The contrast between the Pacer and the just-as-a-customer-would-get-it Corsair was revealing.[15] In the words of *Motor Trend*'s reporter:

> Given nearly idealistic pre-delivery attention by factory mechanics, [the Pacer] showed 186 recorded break-in miles when delivered. Body panels, doors, and windows were perfectly fitted and the paint was excellent both inside and out. Only the hood latch acted up to require a minor adjustment in New Orleans. . . .
>
> Unfortunately, pre-delivery service had not prepared the [Corsair] for cross-country running and it was in and out of three Edsel garages, burnt out one transmission motor (the second began to sag after 2,000 miles), and wore sheet metal that appeared to have been fitted in the dark. . . . Unhappily, the Corsair windshield leaked madly during a rainstorm, as did a yet unfound hole under the dash which filled my left shoe with water.[16]

The reporter went on to note that neither Pacer nor Corsair controls were ever able to completely shut off cold outside air, while the Pacer air intake whistled annoyingly at 50 mph. *Motor Trend*'s reporter loved some features of the two Edsels, however. In particular, he raved about the interior design:

> "What's it like inside?" was a frequently asked question. "Terrific" is the answer which applies equally to either the Pacer or Corsair. . . . Both cars offer exceptional ease of entry and exit. . . . I can't say enough wonderful things about the wonderful seating in the Corsair. . . .
>
> Push buttons are the big news with Edsel's transmission. And believe you me, they are terrific. Last year it took several weeks to find the buttons on my '57 Plymouth, but in only a few hours I was shifting the Edsel without taking my eyes from the road.[17]

On the trip, *Motor Trend* staffers encountered many who loved the Edsel, many who didn't. The latter category included an Edsel owner with "oil leaks, a sticky hood, and trunk he couldn't open." The article's conclusion was tempered:

> With nearly 10,000 miles of serious testing under our trousers, we must admit to still being a little confused about an Edsel's merits. . . . We found that comfort varies greatly between the models, the Pacer provided service while the Corsair needed service much too often, quality is in the

components but not in their assembly or inspection, and, as to beauty. . . .
I believe it's the sharpest car of 1958.[18]

Automotive News, the leading industry trade newspaper, also reported on the
rash of quality control problems with early Edsels, saying that there was an
epidemic of bad paint, poorly fitted or stamped sheet metal, and faulty accessories. The newspaper quoted one unnamed Edsel dealer as reporting the condition of one of the first convertibles the dealer had received: "The top was
badly set, doors cockeyed, the header bar trimmed at the wrong angle, and the
front springs sagged." These sorts of problems were catastrophic for a new
brand seeking to build a reputation. All-important "word-of-mouth" reports
by disgruntled Edsel owners quickly began to tarnish the brand's image.[19]

Equally worrisome, the reaction of the popular press to the Edsel was turning negative. Perhaps the worst early report came courtesy of *Consumer Reports*.
In this era, more so than today, *Consumer Reports* had a marked anti-Detroit
bias. In particular, *Consumer Reports* railed constantly against useless frills, such
as fancy styling, upgraded trim on the more deluxe models, and more powerful engines—in other words, all the "non-essentials" that had been driving the
market since Alfred Sloan cottoned onto them in the 1920s. *Consumer Reports*
would have loved the Model T and this alone made the Edsel Corsair they
tested an unlikely favorite. Still, their reports were read by 800,000 people each
month and couldn't have done the Edsel any good:

> The Edsel has no important basic advantages over other brands. . . . The
> amount of shake in this Corsair body on rough roads—which wasn't long
> in making itself heard as squeaks and rattles—went well beyond any
> acceptable limit. . . . As a matter of simple fact, combined with the car's
> tendency to shake like jelly, Edsel handling represents retrogression rather
> than progress. . . . The center of the steering wheel is not, in CU's opinion,
> a good push button location. . . . The "luxury loaded" Edsel—as one
> magazine cover described it—will certainly please anyone who confuses
> gadgetry with true luxury.[20]

Thus spake *Consumer Reports*. Adding insult to injury, the magazine could-
n't resist taking another swipe in its subsequent 1958 new car issue, calling the
Edsel the "epitome" of the "many excesses" with which Detroit was "repuls-
ing more and more potential car buyers."[21]

Even the car magazines, however, were turning against the Edsel—although for different reasons. For example, one of the other major enthusiast
publications that specialized in Detroit products, *Car Life*, had raved about
the Edsel in its October, 1957 issue:

We liked the Edsels very much. They are smooth, quiet, powerful performers with solid, quality construction, a comfortable ride . . . well-behaved handling characteristics. In the all-important area of styling they have distinctive, pleasing lines. By all the usual indications the Edsel should be a solid hit.[22]

By March of 1958, *Car Life* had changed its tune. That month it ran a banner headline across the top of the magazine asking a question that it is a lead-pipe cinch no one at Ford Motor Company wanted to see on the cover of a publication with national distribution: "Edsel—Ford's Biggest Flop?" Its conclusion:

The big question that remains is whether, after comparing the Edsel . . . with other 1958 models, [American car buyers will] buy enough Edsels to put the car over the sales hump. Ford Motor Company insists that by the end of this spring, it will be clear how the Edsel stacks up against its competitors. By then, we should know whether Edsel is Ford's shining hope for the future or a multi-million dollar financial headache.[23]

One of the most compelling criticisms leveled by *Car Life* was that Ford Motor Company had set its sights too low:

The one point that many automobile executives in Detroit will make, usually off the record, is that Ford stylists certainly missed a chance . . . to design, from the ground up, a really totally new car. There was no styling theme from previous years to be carried out, no owner loyalty to satisfy. But, apparently, Ford Motor Company stylists were not allowed to risk departing from accepted styling trends, for fear of total sales resistance such as Chrysler's Airflow design met in the 1930s. The Edsel designers were saddled with the problem of designing a car which fitted in with the "Ford Family" design. Say auto men: It's a pity, because with a free hand they might have come up with something that would set the auto industry on fire, stir it from its doldrums and—at the same time—put the Edsel over with a big splash.[24]

Car Life, however, also quoted Detroit automakers—off the record—as being convinced that Ford Motor Company would have no choice but to stick with the Edsel. The feeling was that the company would find some way to make it work eventually because the alternative was unthinkable. In fact, as events would prove, the alternative was being thought about quite a lot in the halls of Dearborn . . .

CHAPTER TEN

An early 1959 rendering dated October 12, 1956.

. . . Then Farce

AS SOON AS DESIGN WORK had been completed on the 1958 models—in latter months of 1956—Roy Brown and his team in the Edsel studio began work on the 1959s. Using the face-lifted 1959 Ford and Mercury body shells as a starting point, rough sketches of the new Edsels were prepared and studied. Once the sketches were approved, the building of clay models began.

Early in the development process, a few distinct variations from the 1958 range became apparent. The unique side scallop was removed, and completely new side-trim was designed. The distinctive gullwing tail lights gave way to more conservative clusters of round ones. The Edsel's most unique feature, the "horse collar" grille, although not eliminated, was de-emphasized.

As the design studio labored with body lines and exterior styling changes, the interior designers got to work on trim panels and instrument panel layouts. Their major field of concentration lay, as with the 1958 models, with convenience for the driver. Some of the early ideas passed over—due to lack of technology—on the 1958 models were revived, such as the concept of a wraparound instrument panel. The idea was to place all switches and controls within easy reach of the driver, so that he or she could operate headlights, heater, radio—indeed, any vehicle control device—safely and without removing hands from the steering wheel. Once more, engineering practicality and cost won out. The interior was, accordingly, to be designed around the 1959 Ford instrument panel and cowl, thus limiting the imagination of the designers. How much of what was left was ever going to see the light of day became increasingly problematical as the difficulties encountered by the 1958 Edsel mounted.

What was perhaps the fatal blow was struck on January 14, 1958, with the consolidation of the Edsel Division with Lincoln and Mercury into the new Mercury-Edsel-Lincoln Division (almost invariably referred to as the M-E-L Division, for short). Jim Nance remained in place as general manager for what was really a continuation of the previous Lincoln and Mercury Division under a new name. It was a stunning admission of failure, particularly with regard to the much-trumpeted Edsel, and portended grim times for the new nameplate. In the process, thousands of white collar Edsel Division employees were discharged. Coming on top of the consolidation of Mercury, Lincoln, and Continental divisions the previous year, there was simply no room at the inn for most of the Edsel personnel.

The first Ford Motor Company Annual Report, issued on February 12th, tried to take a positive stance regarding the Edsel. The introductory letter and commentary to the stockholders put it this way:

> The Company's new line of cars, the Edsel, was introduced in September. Edsel sales during the first five months after its introduction did not meet the Company's expectations, primarily because of increasingly adverse conditions which developed in the medium price field. The Company is continuing its efforts to establish the Edsel firmly in the automotive market. Related to such efforts was an organizational move made in early 1958 to unify management direction of the engineering, production and marketing of all the Company's products in the medium and upper price classes. . . . Major moves were made to . . . strengthen the management of the Company's medium and upper-priced car lines. . . . In January, 1958, functions of the Edsel Division were transferred to an expanded division, designated the M-E-L Division.[1]

It was hard to argue with the official reason for the consolidation: Edsel sales simply did not justify the expense of maintaining a separate Edsel Division. The deeper reason was that the McNamara faction, now in the ascendancy, had given up on it. As a practical matter, and despite what the Annual Report suggested about continuing efforts to establish it, after the Edsel was folded into the M-E-L Division there was no longer anyone at Ford Motor Company with a vital interest in seeing it survive. There is a natural dynamic to these things, and it had turned decisively against the Edsel. As Larry Doyle later put it, "With that much competition in a division, the Edsel wasn't going anywhere."[2]

The first sign that the Edsel was being "phased out"—in McNamara's words—was the decision to drastically pare back the 1959 line-up. Almost immediately after the consolidation into the M-E-L Division, the big, Mercury-bodied models were summarily deleted, although the Corsair series designation would end up replacing the Pacer as the top-end Ford-bodied line. McNamara was said to have been personally behind the decision.

Nance, trying his best to keep the Edsel's momentum going—such as it was—issued an upbeat advertisement in February. Placed in *Automotive News*, it was probably intended to buck up sagging dealer morale and restore a little of the Edsel's luster within the industry:

> Since the formation of the new M-E-L Division at Ford Motor Company, we have analyzed with keen interest the sales progress of the Edsel. We think it is quite significant that during the five months since the Edsel was introduced, Edsel sales have been greater than the first five months' sales for any other new make of car ever introduced on the American Road. . . . Edsel's steady progress can be a source of satisfaction and a great incentive to all of us.[3]

Nance, ever sympathetic to the plight of his dealers, instituted an "open door" policy for them. As a result, he was besieged by frantic men who had invested all they had in a brand that was dying—and taking with it the personal fortunes of more men than Nance cared to count. Grown men would sit in his office and weep. Their wives would phone him at home at night. It was almost too much to bear.[4] Desperately, Nance sought to pair Edsel dealers with other M-E-L franchises in order to give them a chance at survival. McNamara insisted that the Edsel dealers could be dualed with Mercury, and generally this was done, but it was not possible in every case.

As winter turned to spring, there was little to provide cheer for those few Edsel loyalists who remained within the M-E-L Division. McNamara's "1960–1961 New Car Interchangeability Program" was revised the first week in June and contained much disheartening news. The stretched Ford body shell was scrubbed and with it any vestige of the Super Mercury concept. The 1961 Mercury tooling budget was therefore reduced a third to $40 million. As for the 1961 Edsel, there was hardly any budget left. A mere $10 million was allocated. Even in 1958 money, that was chump change by Detroit standards. The program noted that "unique [Edsel] parts [will be] limited to hood, quarter panel inserts, grille, bumpers, and exterior ornamentation."[5]

Still, Nance was loathe to give up the cause—at least for public consumption. As late as June, 1958, a lengthy press release was issued in an attempt to rekindle public confidence in the brand. While not denying the all-too-obvious problems the Edsel had suffered, the press release did its best to cast the situation in a positive light, and is worth quoting in its entirety:

> Few business organizations have started life in as difficult a time as the M-E-L Division of Ford Motor Company.
>
> The Division, under the management of James J. Nance, was created January 15, in an atmosphere of falling industry car sales.
>
> Problems were aggravated by the fact that the Edsel—Ford's proud new entry—was in trouble. Seldom had a new car been introduced at a more inauspicious time. Hundreds of millions of dollars had been invested in the Edsel. It was essential that the Edsel "catch on" with the public. Sales were disappointing.
>
> What has happened since that grey day in January? Has the division retreated into a corner to lick its wounds? Has it buried its head in the sand, ostrich-like? And what is the fate of its charge, the Edsel?
>
> The public has learned some of the answers. More are forthcoming.
>
> First task management of the M-E-L Division faced was to pull together all the loose strings, eliminate overlapping departments, bring together personnel who had been working in dozens of separate buildings, set up new lines of management, communication and decision; and, perhaps most importantly, take a fresh look at the situation.
>
> The first steps were accomplished quickly. The last took a little more time, because the nation's economy was spiraling downward and the situation changed daily.
>
> The automobile industry was taking its lumps. Everyone who was anyone—and a few who weren't—became vocal critics of the industry and lectured Detroit on what should be done.
>
> The Edsel, because of its newness on the American scene, because also of its very different styling, became the scapegoat. A few critics already were spading dirt on Edsel's grave.
>
> To put the situation in sports terms, M-E-L was on its five-yard line and the opposition was charging through. A quarterback might be tempted to fall on the ball and hope time ran out in the first half.
>
> With the Division barely more than a month old, Mr. Nance took to the field for a series of "cold turkey" meetings with Edsel dealers. They took heart, redoubled their sales efforts.
>
> Edsel sales began perking up.
>
> A person versed in books might describe Edsel's life history to that point in terms of these titles: "Great Expectations," "The Gathering Storm," "The Crisis," and "The Road Back."
>
> Edsel has passed "The Crisis," and is on "The Road Back."

Momentum brought Edsel sales to a low in February. The upturn began in March and has continued to this date, passing the 50,000 mark in total sales in June.

In terms of total industry sales of millions of cars each year, sales of 50,000 Edsels may not seem particularly significant. But,when matched against the sales figures of other cars in their first year on the market, Edsel sales are remarkable. Particularly in this recession year. Seen in this perspective, Edsel is doing well.

A record is within Edsel's reach for any first-year car in its price class, and now Edsel is shooting for the all-time first-year sales record set by a low-priced make in a high-volume year.

For example, Edsel marked its 50,965th sale June 30, passing the first year sales of 50,629 for Pontiac, introduced in 1926, and 19,960 made by Chrysler which appeared on the market in 1924. Mr. Nance said that when Edsel completes its first model year, it will probably have outsold De Soto's 54,249 (introduced in 1928), and Mercury's 58,590 (introduced in 1938). Edsel's target now is the 75,536 record established by Plymouth in its introductory model year of 1928.

Edsel's strong first-year start is a good indication of its future in the most competitive market in the world. How competitive it is shown by the gravestones along the trail blazed by the industry that has transformed the way America lives, travels, works and thinks.

In such relentless competition, the mortality of new cars is high. Here is the death roll of cars introduced since 1938 and no longer with us: Aerocar (1948), Bobbie Kar (1947), Davis (1945), Del Mar (1949), Frazer (1946), Gregory (1948), Henry J (1950), Hoppenstand (1948), Kaiser (1947), Keller (1947), Muntz (1950), Mustang (1948), Playboy (1947), Publix (1947), Pup (1948), Rocket (1946), Towne Shopper (1948), Tucker (1947), and Willys-American (1940). Only eighteen basic automobile makes survived the 1,686 different cars that have been produced and put on the market since the industry began replacing the horse. And, since Mercury was introduced in 1938, at least twenty-five other makes of cars have appeared.

Only three, the Mercury, Edsel and Continental, still are on the market. All three are the responsibility of the M-E-L Division.[6]

In fact, the Edsel's first year production amounted to a mere 63,110 units. The 1959 Edsel line-up, when it finally appeared in the fall of 1958, was pared back both in numbers of models and in price range. In truth, the 1959 Edsel was little more than a deluxe Ford.

In an effort to maintain some of the class distinction of the Mercury-bodied EM series, the Pacer series became the Corsair, which was now the top of the Edsel line. The Corsair line included two- and four-door hardtops, a four-door

sedan, and a two-door convertible. The economy series was still the Ranger, offered in two- and four-door hardtops, and two- and four-door sedans. The only
entry in the station wagon class, the Villager, was produced with either six- or
nine-passenger seating arrangements.

The Edsel Express V8, a carryover from 1958, was the standard engine for the
Corsair line and the Villager station wagon, and was optional for the Ranger.
The standard Ranger 292-cubic-inch V8 was available only on the Ranger
line. The standard transmission for all lines was the manual three-speed, with
either a two- or three-speed automatic optional. Gone, however, were the
push buttons; all automatic transmission-equipped Edsels for 1959 used a column shifter.

The only performance option was the 361-cubic-inch V8 carried over from
1958. This engine was available only with an automatic transmission. For the
economy-minded, the Edsel Economy Six was an option on the Ranger and
Villager. This engine was a proven Ford six-cylinder displacing 223 cubic
inches. A full range of accessories was offered, as well, though little that was
unique to the Edsel.

The automotive press virtually ignored the 1959 Edsel. Ironically, *Consumer
Reports*, which had savaged the 1958 edition, decided it liked the watered-down
1959 line quite a lot. A review noted, in part:

> Ford . . . after giving last year's initial Edsel model a black eye, has made a
> respectable and even likable automobile of it. . . . And if the Corsair is
> basically a Ford, this is not necessarily a shortcoming. There is very little in
> this Edsel of the hasty-pudding designing which afflicted the 1958 models.[7]

Tragically, the Edsel dealer body reached its highest point in 1959, with 1,568
signed on as of February. They signed on just in time to read the first rumors
of the Edsel's demise in the nation's press. These began as early as the spring of
1959 and were to increase in intensity as the year dragged on, spurred by the
Edsel's declining sales figures. During the 1959 model run, a total of 44,891
units were produced.

Nance didn't survive to see the launch of the 1959 models. McNamara finally
managed to have him fired in August, 1958. According to Nance, the Whiz
Kids had given Henry Ford II an ultimatum: fire him or the Whiz Kids would
desert Ford Motor Company in a group for a lucrative job offer at Chrysler.[8]

It was Ernie Breech's swan song, too. He was soon kicked upstairs to the
"honorary" chairmanship of the board, while Henry II assumed the chairmanship and McNamara became president. The Whiz Kids had vanquished
the product men, and Ford Motor Company would never be the same.

On this and the following two pages are early renderings of possible 1959 front end treatments. All are from the latter part of 1956 and are dated between August 24th and October 12th. In the studio, they were mounted upon a "storyboard" like the one shown at the bottom of the third page.

... THEN FARCE

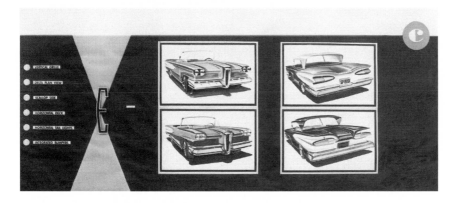

At right, an early clay with preliminary 1959 rear-end development that continues the 1958 gull-wing theme. *Below,* two views of a Mercury-based clay dated December, 1956. One side is a Ranger series two-door hardtop, the other side is a Caravan series four-door hardtop.

Approval clays for the Ford-bodied 1959 models. The Pacer
is fairly close in general lines to the production car, except
for the side trim.

Approval clays for the Mercury-bodied 1959 models. The big Corsair hardtop (*top and middle*) and Citation convertible (*bottom*) never made it because that body was scrapped.

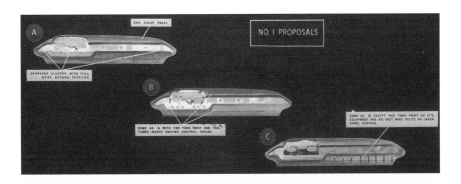

Various 1959 station wagon and interior design development examples.

The design center photo session numbers place these models well after the 1959 design was finalized and show a wide-ranging attempt to explore alternative grille themes typical of a design team in the early stages of development of a product. Were they early 1960 model studies? Two shots (*first row right, second row left*) show the vertical bar theme almost used in 1960. Another two shots (*third row, fourth row right*) are supposedly the 1959 Pacer approval model, but show a front end that bears no resemblance to the actual car, so who knows?

A Corsair two-door hardtop.

A Corsair four-door sedan.

A Corsair four-door hardtop.

A Corsair convertible.

A Ranger two-door hardtop.

A Ranger two-door sedan.

A Ranger four-door hardtop.

A Ranger four-door sedan.

A Ranger rear end.

A Villager station wagon (front view).

A Villager (rear view).

CHAPTER ELEVEN

1960 Edsel Ranger four-door sedan.

Final Act . . . and Curtain

BY THE TIME THE 1960 MODELS went into final development, the Edsel, which had started life as one of the most rigorously planned and fussed-over projects in history, one over which virtually anyone who counted at Ford Motor Company had an intense interest, had become an unwanted stepchild. Indeed, it is arguable that the man who had the most influence—at least indirectly—on the 1960 Edsel was not an employee of Ford Motor Company at all. That man was Virgil M. Exner, chief designer at Chrysler. To understand Exner's influence on what was destined to be the final Edsel series, a little history is in order.

Exner had a long and eventful career in the auto industry. Following a stint at General Motors, where he was largely responsible for the design of the 1937 and 1938 Pontiacs, Exner joined Studebaker's design staff under Raymond Loewy. There, he played a key role in creating the striking 1947 Studebakers, the first all-new postwar cars from any major manufacturer. On the strength of that achievement, he was hired away by Chrysler in 1949.

Chrysler, which, as has been noted, had elevated dowdiness to an art form in the 1940s, desperately needed a man of Exner's flair. For the first several years he was at Chrysler, however, Exner was given little latitude to exercise his considerable talents. Then, Chrysler's products went into a collective tail-spin in 1953. Suddenly shocked back to reality, Chrysler management borrowed tens of millions of dollars and gave Exner the green light for a crash program to design an entirely new line of Chrysler products for 1955. When these cars were a big success, management told Exner to do it again for 1957 and, this time, Exner decided to pull out all the stops.

Looking back, the Chrysler "Forward Look" cars of 1957 were the post–World War II high watermark of Chrysler Corporation as an auto producer. Although remembered today for their gargantuan tail fins, they were breath-taking in their clean lines, flat hoods that rested far below the fender lines, expanded use of glass for light, airy greenhouses, the industry's first use of curved side window glass on some models, dramatic wedge shapes, and, on most lines, restrained use of chrome. The Plymouth slogan that year—"Suddenly It's 1960!"—was more than just the product of an over-eager copy writer's imagination. It was true. Chrysler was suddenly setting the design standard for the industry.

The people at Ford weren't excessively bothered by this at first; they had impressive new Fords and Mercurys for 1957, and dramatic new Thunderbird, Edsel, and Lincoln lines in the works for 1958. Most of these turned out to be (in varying degrees) flops, of course, although Ford management couldn't have known it in 1956. General Motors' people, however, and especially the younger designers, were stunned.

The Olds, Buick, and Cadillac B- and C-bodies were new for 1957, the new Chevy and Pontiac A-body was already locked-up for 1958—and they all looked like your grandmother's corset next to a 1957 Plymouth. Indeed, they looked almost as bad next to a 1957 Ford Fairlane 500. General Motors executives were beside themselves even before the sales reports started coming in. They broke into a panic when Ford pulled solidly ahead of Chevy in registrations as the new model selling season opened in the fall of 1956. Ford hadn't made that kind of a breakthrough since 1935. Something had to be done—and fast.

A Pontiac internal engineering report written by Assistant Chief Engineer J. P. Charles, and issued after the development of the 1959 models, assessed the situation dryly:

> The trend toward lower and longer cars was being accelerated by the intense competition in the lower-priced field. Competition outside General Motors was styled in slimmer, crisper lines, with some restraint in the use of chrome; and this styling trend was meeting with good public acceptance.[1]

It was, indeed. In fact, shortly after the New York Auto Show in December, 1956, the corporate decision was made that all General Motors lines, from

An early 1960 clay for the Ranger/Pacer series. At this point, the 1960 Edsel was still scheduled to be built on the 1959 Ford body shell.

Chevrolet to Cadillac, should have completely new bodies for 1959. And . . . this is where the plot thickens. Ford management, while they hadn't been especially bothered by the 1957 Chrysler products, went into a panic of their own when they saw what was going on at arch-rival Chevy.

By January of 1958—a few months into the 1958 model year—Ford Motor Company was, in fact, rocked by a couple of unexpected, but related, developments. First, the revised Ford line, which had clobbered Chevy in 1957, wasn't repeating the performance. In fact, Chevy, was pulling solidly into the lead in sales on the strength of an all-new, larger, and (some thought) handsomer 1958 design. That was worrisome enough to McNamara, but he and his colleagues at Ford Division were astonished when they learned of General Motors' crash program for the 1959 model run due only a few months down the road. Chevrolet would have yet another entirely new line of cars! Two years in a row! It was hard to believe, but, like it or not, Ford was forced to suddenly reconsider its options in order to determine what—if anything—could be done in response.

Therefore, with Chevrolet firmly in mind, McNamara took a long look at the then-current 1960 Ford proposal. The vehicle was to be face-lifted yet again from the 1957–59 Ford body shell, with a redesigned cast grille and new wedge-shaped tail lights. Although he knew that the already finalized 1959 Ford was much-improved over the one Chevy was beating in 1958, it was still higher, narrower and boxier than what Ford believed they could expect from Chevrolet in 1959. While McNamara didn't have time to do anything about the 1959 car—the train had already left the station on that one—he became convinced that the 1960 line should be lower and sleeker than anything possible from the 1957–59 body shell. So, to the surprise of the designers, he ordered that all work be stopped on the 1960 design and that they immediately create another vehicle with lines that would afford it equal footing with Chevy in the low-priced market.

As it happened, a new Ford following the general design trend (minus the fins) launched by Chrysler with its Forward Look had been in the works for the 1961 model year. This is where the story becomes ambiguous. Touring the advanced design studios one day, according to one version, McNamara ran across an old concept vehicle lying covered and forgotten in a secluded corner. Designed strictly as an advanced, futuristic vehicle to be shown only at car shows, it had been used for that purpose, then returned to the studio and forgotten. "La Galaxie," as it was called, drew McNamara's attention. He questioned the studio staff about it and demanded that the cover be removed to allow him to view it. After a rapid glance, he informed the staff that it was to be the basis for the 1960 Ford and departed.

The other version of the story contends that McNamara simply ordered the existing 1961 design, already under way (and perhaps heavily influenced by La Galaxie), to be pulled forward a year. Or, perhaps some combination of the two. In any case, Ford Division scrapped its nearly finished 1960 design and instituted a crash development program reminiscent of General Motors' experience with its 1959s. Barely a year and a half remained before the 1960 Fords were due to be announced to the public, half the normal new model development time.

It was at virtually the same juncture that McNamara also ordered the formation of the Mercury-Edsel-Lincoln (M-E-L) Division. Then, three months later, the Edsel, having lost its divisional status, lost half its model range as the corporation's plans for it continued to contract. The larger, Mercury-bodied Corsair and Citation were scrapped, reducing the 1960 Edsel to a variation of the 1960 Ford, with only distinctive front- and rear-end themes to call its own.

After the 1957–59-based 1960 Ford and Edsel were scrapped, Bob Jones, now design chief due to Roy Brown's transfer to the truck studio, began to adapt a 1960 Edsel from the new La Galaxie-based 1960 Ford. The resulting Edsel, planned in 1959 to include Ranger and Corsair lines, was even less distinct from the Ford than before. The vertical grille was only a suggestion, consisting of a thin, chrome bar in the center of the same grille cavity the Edsel essentially shared with Ford. In back, vertical tail lights and back-up lights repeated the theme. Other than that, only a few trim pieces differentiated the 1960 Edsel from the 1960 Ford in a way that gave the new Edsel any identity at all. At least it was something. Soon, however, it was to be reduced to almost nothing.

One evening, shortly before the final approval of the 1960 Edsel and on the eve of departing for England, Ernie Breech, who was still Ford's chairman, made a tour of the Edsel studio. Viewing Jones' completed prototype, Breech expressed his dislike in no uncertain terms, objecting to the vertical grille even in vestigial form. He instructed Jones to remove it and refashion a front end similar to the split grille theme of the 1959 Pontiac, then the hottest car in the medium-priced field. Jones wasn't given much time; the changes had to be re-worked in time for Breech's inspection the next morning. Working through the night, Jones removed the vertical bar and fashioned a new center grille insert that mimicked the Pontiac theme. Breech approved it.[2]

Now that the new car didn't even look like an Edsel, the model range was reduced yet again. At the last minute, the Corsair series was dropped, leaving only the Ranger (and related Villager wagons). Some accounts contend that there was talk of reviving the Citation series, but this idea, too, was abandoned prior to production.

The Ranger was more or less divided into a couple of series, though, dependent upon interior trim, of which there were two variations offered. One was a standard interior featuring fabric trim; the other featured a combination Champagne Cloth-and-Moroccan Vinyl deluxe trim in various colors. The EA Ranger was produced with the standard interior and included two- or four-door sedan, and two-door hardtop body styles. Within the corporation, the EB Rangers were delivered with the deluxe trim and included two- and four-door hardtop, and convertible body styles. The EB Rangers were unofficially referred to as Corsairs. The Villager station wagon was once more packaged as either a six- or nine-passenger model. The standard power team on all models was the carryover 1959 Ranger 292-cubic-inch V8 with manual three-speed transmission. Performance options were the 352-cubic-inch Super Express V8 and either two- or three-speed automatic transmissions.

There was supposed to have been an Edsel compact car for 1960, as well—the Edsel Comet—and thereby hangs still another tale. The genesis of the Comet dates back to the mid-1950s when compact cars first began to make an impact on the American market. General Motors, Ford, and Chrysler had been engaged off and on with small car programs since the 1930s. None of the programs ever came to anything, though, and there was no guarantee that this effort would, either.

What tipped the balance was the explosion in buyer demand for smaller cars in the latter years of the decade. Volkswagen was starting to gain prominence and, then, in 1958, the American Motors Rambler suddenly took off. In 1959, Studebaker joined the fray with its Lark and it was assumed that the Big Three could not be far behind. The first Big Three compacts—the Chevrolet

Corvair, the Ford Falcon, and the Plymouth Valiant—all appeared in the latter months of 1959 for the 1960 model year. By 1961, Buick, Olds, Pontiac, Dodge, and Mercury all fielded compacts of their own, as well.

In April of 1958, Ford Division had presented the "Ford Economy Car Program" to, and received approval from, the board of directors for the 1960 Ford XK Thunderbird (later renamed the Falcon). The following month, a similar program, code-named Canberra, was initiated by the M-E-L Division. The M-E-L Division made its preliminary presentation to the Ford product planning committee in July, 1958, outlining the use of the Ford XK Thunderbird as a basis for an Edsel compact. Also proposed was sufficient product value to allow higher pricing than the Ford version. The final program was presented to the product planning committee in September, 1958, duly approved, and code-named the 1961 Edsel B.

According to reliable reports, the Edsel B was in fact approved as a replacement for—not as an addition to—the full-size Edsel line scheduled for 1961. For example, the respected industry trade magazine *Automotive Industries* reported in its October 15, 1959, issue:

> Ford Motor Co. officials have confirmed earlier reports in *Automotive Industries* of a second compact car. This one is to be called "Comet" and will be marketed next spring by M-E-L dealers. . . . Comet was designated as Edsel B throughout its development stage. It is scheduled to replace the full-sized Edsel after the 1960 model year.[3]

It made sense. Mercury was going to be downgraded to the Ford body shell effective with the 1961 model year. Since most surviving Edsel dealers had, by this time, been paired up with Lincoln-Mercury, there was obviously little room for two Ford-based lower-medium-priced lines in the same showroom. M-E-L dealers would, however, need a compact in order to be competitive, so repositioning the Edsel as the M-E-L compact line at least gave it a plausible role to play (and, arguably, for the first time, too).

In the end, nothing related to the 1960 or 1961 Edsel programs turned out even remotely as planned. The final act of the Edsel was perhaps the last, convoluted result of the Forward Look saga around which so many ironies abounded. Chrysler, which had started the whole panic with its dramatically new 1957 designs, all but destroyed its once enviable reputation for engineering excellence due to the unspeakably shoddy quality of many of the cars actually built. Chrysler corporately soared to better than 18 percent in market share in 1957, only to tumble to barely 11 percent by 1959—a more dreadful level of penetration than the one that had prompted the Forward Look campaign in the first place. General Motors, which turned itself inside out attempting to match the Wonders from Highland Park, saw most of its 1959 nameplates languish, including Chevrolet—for whom the battle was primarily waged. Ford, which mounted its own crash program to keep up with General Motors' crash response to Chrysler, stumbled badly, as well. The "old" 1959 Fords outsold the new Chevys, while the new 1960 Fords faltered in the marketplace, at the same time engendering exactly the sort of problems Chrysler had faced back in 1957 due to poor quality resulting from rushed production.

But . . . there was still more. No one at Pontiac, it seems, appreciated the impact the split grille would have; it was just a styling device like any other to them. When it caught on big with the public, Pontiac designers were caught totally flat-footed with a 1960 front-end design in the can that abandoned the theme. It was 1961 before the split returned at Pontiac.

So, in 1960, anyone who wanted a split grille had to buy an Edsel. Few buyers availed themselves of the opportunity, however, or had much opportunity to avail themselves of it. The 1960 Edsels were formally introduced on October 15, 1959, and the last vehicle bearing the name came down the line barely a month later on November 19th. Only 2,846 had been built.

Curiously, the demise of Ford Motor Company's most conspicuously ambitious failure of the postwar era wasn't formally announced until after the press had got wind of it from a source outside the company. The word came in the fine print of a prospectus issued by the Ford Foundation, a document legally required in order to sell two million shares of the Ford stock the foundation held. By law, the prospectus was required to state the future business plans of the company. Clearly, the Edsel was no longer a part of those plans. The prospectus listed the brands being built by the company as Ford, Mercury, and Lincoln. In a footnote, it was explained that the Edsel had been "introduced in September, 1957, and discontinued in November, 1959."[4]

Ironically, the foundation had also been the source of the first hard news of the company's intention to launch the Edsel. Back in December, 1955, in another prospectus, the foundation had been forced to list the E-Car as part of the future business plans of the company. So, it had come full circle. The Ford Foundation had heralded the birth of the Edsel and announced its death, as well.

Moreover, press reports at the time went so far as to state that the timing of the Edsel's discontinuation was forced by the foundation's dilemma. In other words, it was felt that dumping the Edsel would boost the price of the stock and benefit the foundation. Conversely, not noting the possibility of the Edsel's demise could have gotten the foundation into hot water with the Securities and Exchange Commission (SEC). Henry II, who was a power in the

foundation as well as in the company, could not have been unaware of this—
or of the implications.

In any event, the company was forced to make a decision. The official announcement from the company tried to put the best face on it:

> Following introduction by the automobile industry of its 1960 models, in
> cluding the economy cars, retail sales of the new Edsel have been particularly
> disappointing and considerably below sales in the periods following 1958 and
> 1959 model introductions.
>
> Favorable public response to all other Ford Motor Company lines, how
> ever, was immediate. Retail sales of Lincolns, Mercurys, Fords, Falcons,
> Thunderbird and Continentals increased in the first 10 days of November
> more than 40 percent above the same period a year ago. In total, these six
> Ford Motor Company car lines accounted for 33 percent of all industry retail
> sales, including foreign imports, for the first 10 days of November.
>
> In view of this high consumer preference for other company lines and the
> severe decline in the demand for Edsel cars, the continued production of the
> Edsel is not justified, especially in view of the shortage of steel, the effects of
> which will extend into 1960. Even the relatively small amount of steel, manu
> facturing facilities and related employment used in current Edsel production,
> when diverted to other company models, will help meet the strong consumer
> demand of those car lines.
>
> Accordingly, Edsel production will be halted and the Edsel discontinued as
> a product of Ford Motor Company.[5]

A grand total of eighteen Edsels came down the line on November 19th, the
last cars to bear the nameplate. Commented a company official, "They were
special orders, although now I don't know whether the buyers will want them."[6]
Actually, the remaining 1960 Edsels turned out to be fairly hot commodities.
The company had moved quickly on November 20th to announce a $300 rebate to any owner of a 1960 Edsel toward the purchase of another Ford product. Dealers were also offered a $400 rebate on the 1,344 new Edsels remaining
in factory or dealer hands, as well as on any 1959 models still unsold. The two
rebates were not cumulative—they couldn't both be used on a single car purchase—but they served to clear out remaining stocks in short order.

Of the 1,468 remaining Edsel dealers, all but two were dualed with either
Ford or Lincoln-Mercury by that point, and so could soldier on with relatively
little inconvenience. As for Ford Motor Company, of the $250 million invested
in the Edsel program, perhaps a much as $150 million went into plants and facilities that remained assets to the company. It was estimated that operational
losses during the life of the Edsel cost the company around $100 million, making a final loss of around $200 million, or more than $1,800 per car.

Then, in a postscript—and as if adding insult to injury—the most successful Edsel of all, the Comet, was built as a Mercury. The Mercury Comet was virtually indistinguishable from the Edsel version; only the name had been changed, as they say, to protect the innocent. The Comet, in Mercury guise, was announced to the public on March 17, 1960. A grand total of 116,331 were built during the few months the series was on sale in the 1960 model run. This was more than total Edsel production in all three model years combined (110,810) and one is left to wonder what the future of the Edsel might have been had the brand somehow survived long enough to sire its compact offspring.

The earliest 1960 Edsel design efforts begin on this page. *Left and below* are two themes being tried on one car. *Bottom* is an early Ranger/Pacer study from Ford's advanced studio.

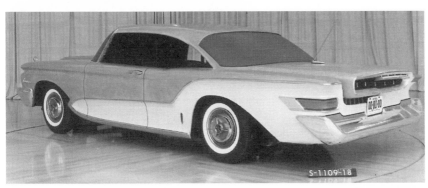

Top is the rear of an early Ranger/Pacer Ford-based clay on the 1959 Ford body shell that also appears on page 169. *The middle two* clays are a Corsair based on the Mercury body shell. *Bottom* is a 1960 Corsair/Citation proposal, according to the design center photo numbers.

Various front and rear-end design studies appear on this and the next page. All are based on the 1959 Ford body shell. *Top* is an early effort that looks a lot like the actual 1959 production car. The split grille was explored long before the final 1960 design was done. The rear-end clays explore 1959-ish themes that were later discarded. The one at the *bottom* is probably the same car shown at the bottom of the previous page.

More front and rear-end design studies based on the 1959 Ford body shell.

This and the next page, final clays on the actual 1960 Ford body shell. *Top*, the earliest front-end treatment is a continuation of the split grille concepts started on the 1959 body shell. *Bottom*, a further development begins to show the front end as it actually appeared. Note the thin, vertical grille bar that did not make it to production.

More final clays on the actual 1960 Ford body shell. The photos on this page show a variety of rear-end treatments.

On this page are several proposal for the stillborn Corsair. Since few stampings differed from the Ford, it required lots of trim to make it look different.

Top, the final instrument cluster and what was supposed to have been the final front treatment. The 1959 Pontiac look, *bottom*, came at the last minute.

On this page, the Edsel Comet. *Top*, the earliest clay looks a lot like the Canadian Falcon equivalent, the Frontenac. *Bottom*, an early frontal treatment.

More clays of the Edsel Comet. *Top*, one closer to the production car (except for the vertical bar). *Middle*, the rear end takes shape using tail lights similar to those on the big Edsel, but canted. The clay on the *bottom* is close to the production car.

On this page and the next one, production 1960 Edsels. *Top*, the Villager station wagon. *Bottom*, the final steering wheel and gauge cluster.

More production 1960 Edsels. *Top*, another view of the Villager station wagon.
Middle, the Ranger two-door hardtop. *Bottom*, the trunk of the Ranger sedan.
The same car appears as an opening shot for this chapter.

Two more 1960 production cars. *Top*, a Ranger sedan. *Bottom*, the Ranger convertible. The convertible was the rarest of all 1960 Edsels.

CHAPTER TWELVE

1960 Mercury Comet.

Why the Edsel Failed

IF FORD MOTOR COMPANY had long since given up on the Edsel, it was extremely concerned, nonetheless, about the potential public and press response to the official announcement of that fact. A detailed report was, therefore, ordered and completed by January of 1960. The report was surprisingly upbeat, and stated in part:

> Results were better than might have been expected. First-day wire service stories and specials—the ones which made the biggest splash—were factual and contained a minimum of potentially harmful interpretation. Play was restrained and first-day stories appeared in inside pages of 44 percent of papers sampled; follow-up stories were almost exclusively inside. . . . References to the one plus in the company statement—about favorable public response to other Ford Motor Company car lines—were numerous and prominent; emphasis on rebates for dealers and allowances for customers also was favorable. Editorials were sympathetic in the main and many contained important plugs for the company and its products. The inevitable column banter was tempered by friendly farewells and expressions of understanding. . . . Headline treatment was predominantly restrained and factual. A few papers used such harsh terms as "Flop," "Scuttles," "Scraps," "Ditches"

and "Junks," but the vast majority preferred "Drops," "Halts," "Stops," "Discontinues" and the semi-mild "Abandons."[1]

As if to prove that statistical analysis was alive and well at the company, the report noted that of 334 stories based on AP or UPI wire service material sampled, 304 were "mild" (i.e., essentially favorable to the company) and only 30 were "strong" (i.e., negative). Of all stories sampled, 277 headlines were one column wide, 73 were two columns wide, and 26 were three columns or wider. Only three newspapers—the *Detroit News*, the *Chicago Daily News*, and the *Springfield* (Massachusetts) *News*—made it their front-page "banner" story.

The only major publication singled out as being openly hostile to the company was *Time* magazine:

> With characteristic scorn, *Time* headed its story, "The $250 Million Flop," called the company announcement "pained," and concluded: "The Edsel was a classic case of the wrong car for the wrong market at the wrong time. It also was a prime example of the limitations of market research, with its 'in-depth interviews' and 'motivational' mumbo-jumbo." *Time* also couldn't resist repeating a bromide, saying, "Edsel's styling, in particular the grille, which resembled an Oldsmobile sucking a lemon, was not much help, even after the lemon was removed."

The report concluded that, of course, the company would have "gladly given up" all the favorable treatment "for not having had to make the Edsel announcement at all," but noted:

> Having to announce the discontinuance of an automobile is an unpleasant task. The news is negative to begin with and the history of the Edsel was such that it already had been the butt of countless jokes, and its early departure had been predicted repeatedly. As a *Wall Street Journal* man remarked, the final announcement marked merely the throwing of the last shovelful of dirt on a clearly labeled grave.
>
> So, we started from nothing. We said we had a failure on our hands, admitted we'd made a mistake. We made the point as strongly as we could that the performance of the Edsel was not to be confused with that of our other lines, which were doing splendidly—but in a way that served merely to emphasize what a flop the Edsel really was. . . .
>
> Taken as a whole, though . . . publicity on the Edsel's death was dominated by a sincere effort on the part of most media to be friendly and sympathetic. Maybe it was simply the traditional respect for the dead . . . however, we are justified in assuming that the reaction of the press reflects a basically friendly attitude toward the company, its products, its founder, and Ford's half-century of contributions to the nation.

Beginning on the day of the announcement and continuing in diminishing volume—but apparently without end—over the years, there were any number of reasons advanced to explain why the Edsel failed. Ford Motor Company conspicuously declined to join the fun. Noted a company spokesman: "If we knew the reason people aren't buying the Edsel, we'd probably have done something about it."[2] Still, there had to be a reason (or reasons). The major suggestions will be considered below. Some of these "reasons" played a major role, indeed, while some—including several of the ones most widely believed — are, in reality, little more than popular misconceptions.

THE DIFFICULTY OF LAUNCHING ANY NEW BRAND

This was an early theme in press obituaries for the Edsel. It is certainly true that such a task is fraught with many perils. Henry Kaiser, whose own automotive venture had failed about the time the Edsel was launched and was something of an expert on the subject, said: "We expected to toss $50 million into the automotive pond; we didn't expect it to disappear without a ripple."[3] As noted automotive publisher Floyd Clymer remarked in his *World on Wheels* magazine:

> Ford Motor Company need not feel too badly about its quick decision to abandon Edsel. Every automobile concern now in business has abandoned makes and models in past years. General Motors Corporation leads the group of firms that have abandoned cars which became orphans.

The death of the Edsel also revived speculation about the future of Chrysler's De Soto brand, and even about General Motors' Pontiac. Both companies were forced to issue heated denials, although the De Soto was, in fact, gone within the year in a near repeat of the Edsel's demise (even including rebates for those unfortunate enough to have bought De Sotos near the end). Noted the *Detroit News*:

> The [Edsel] decision . . . emphasizes again what a tremendous gamble the automobile business really is. . . . The industry is less a gamble than it was fifty years ago, but a great element of chance still remains and the manufacturers need luck as well as skill and salesmanship.

Of course, noting that the job is difficult hardly helps much to explain why Ford Motor Company failed—unless one assumes that failure was preordained in any such attempt. Through the years, Ford, General Motors, and Chrysler have all demonstrated the contrary. Indeed, General Motors was to prove it again in recent times with the launch of the Saturn, while Toyota and Nissan have further proven the point with the successful launches of their Lexus and Infiniti brands, respectively.

THE TIMING

Timing, as the saying goes, is everything. Many of the reasons offered for the failure of the Edsel cited, in one way or another, the unarguably bad timing of the project.

When the Edsel was planned, the medium-priced market was booming. By the time the Edsel was announced, however, the industry, in general, was reeling and the medium-priced segment was hit worst of all. Many of the post-mortems on the Edsel—especially those written at the time of the demise— faulted the company for expanding in the wrong direction, i.e., launching a medium-priced car in 1958 instead of a compact. With remarkable foresight, the *Bergen Evening Record* in the New Jersey suburbs of New York City even suggested the Japanese car invasion when it characterized the company's actions as a "stubbornly shortsighted giveaway to manufacturers in Germany, Sweden, France, Italy, and now even Japan."

As was noted in Chapter Nine, the 3 million cars sold in the medium-priced field in 1955 collapsed to barely 1.2 million by 1958, a drop of 60 percent in three years. Every mid-price competitor suffered. Among the General Motors trio that was the prime competition for the Edsel, Buick declined 64 percent, Pontiac declined 57 percent, and Oldsmobile, showing the "best" performance of the General Motors brands in that segment, declined a mere 48 percent. Worse, Buick, Olds, and Pontiac had traditionally supplied 45–50 percent of General Motors' unit volume; by 1958, the Buick-Olds-Pontiac (B-O-P) share had fallen to 37 percent and was still shrinking. And, they were the lucky ones. Some major brands didn't survive at all. No less than five medium-priced name-plates went under between 1957 and 1960: Nash and Hudson (1957), Packard (1958), Edsel (1959), and De Soto (1960). There is anecdotal evidence that General Motors considered dropping Pontiac, too.

Quite simply, the Edsel's timing was atrocious. The launch, originally scheduled for June or July, 1957, might have helped at first, but there was no way 1958 was going to turn out to be a propitious time to introduce a medium-priced car. This was no one's fault, to be sure. Lead times being what they are in the auto industry, a company always runs the risk that the market may change dramatically before a new product hits the streets. It is a danger that causes problems with some frequency, but the Edsel is clearly a worst-case scenario. The *Atlanta Journal* focused in on this problem in its obituary:

> If Ford had first manufactured the Edsel ten years ago, it might have been the hottest thing on the market. On the other hand, had the [Kaiser-built] Henry J emerged as a new 1960 compact car, it might have succeeded. The potential was there in both ventures. But, as is the case in many instances, timing is the difference between a pop-up and a home run.

THE ANTI-DETROIT ATTITUDE AMONG THE PUBLIC

The 1958 model year was not only a terrible one for the medium-priced field, however; the industry was reeling almost across the board. Only one brand recorded a gain: Rambler. Everyone else was down. Many of the articles in the popular press fingered growing dissatisfaction with Detroit as a prime culprit.

George Romney, head of American Motors, added fuel to the fire with his aggressive Rambler advertising campaign in which it was cleverly depicted as a common sense, socially responsible alternative to the gas hog dinosaurs being built by Detroit. The boom in compact cars was on and Romney's Rambler—the big success story of the year—only served to underscore the growing popular view of Detroit as being woefully out of touch with its customers.

The enthusiast press jumped on the bandwagon, as well. *Road & Track* had made a name for itself in this era by extolling the virtues of foreign cars and attacking everything that was "wrong" with Detroit iron, but suddenly even "establishment" magazines such as *Motor Trend* were joining in. In its October, 1957, issue—the same one that introduced the Edsel to its readers—the lead feature in *Motor Trend* was an article entitled, "What's wrong with U.S. cars?" The article missed no opportunity to attack virtually everything about them. "The root trouble with American automobiles," the article ranted, "would seem to be that they are now designed primarily by the stylists and fashion experts, while European cars are built by engineers and drivers."[4] Presumably, American automakers had fired all their engineers and the stylists didn't know how to drive.

John Keats' celebrated book, *Insolent Chariots*, was published around this time, too, and was only one of a slew of books and articles hostile to Detroit "culture" that flooded the popular market. It was also about this time that Vance Packard published his influential book, *The Hidden Persuaders*. Packard's ostensible target was Madison Avenue. He attacked the ethics of the advertising fraternity—an oxymoron?—asserting that they manipulated the public into buying things that weren't really wanted or needed. It was all something of a fraud, according to Packard, and all major purveyors of consumer products got tarnished in the process.

As was noted in Chapter Nine, David Wallace, one of the division's product planners, pinpointed the demise of the Edsel from October 4, 1957—the day Sputnik went into orbit. Anyone alive at that time will recall the emotional shock Sputnik caused on the American psyche. Suddenly America wasn't the unrivaled leader, and, overnight, Americans began to question the quality of almost everything about their society. Science, business, government, education, and American culture itself were suddenly suspect. To the extent that the Edsel depended for its success upon American car buyers lusting after their rolling piece of the American Dream, any questioning of the validity of that dream can't have benefited the Edsel.

Larry Doyle likewise put the blame for the Edsel's failure squarely on popular revulsion with Detroit. He said later:

> It was a buyer's strike. People weren't in the mood for the Edsel. . . . What they'd been buying for several years encouraged the industry to build exactly this kind of car. We gave it to them, and they wouldn't take it.[5]

In short, it was a bad time for the images of Detroit and consumer products businesses, in general. To the degree that the Edsel was dependent upon public confidence in one of the largest consumer products producers in America—i.e., Ford Motor Company—the national mood cannot have helped. How badly it may have hurt the Edsel, though, is impossible to say.

Ironically, the demise of the Edsel seems to have played a significant role in debunking the idea that consumers were but so many sheep ripe for the shearing. *The Wall Street Journal* noted:

> All this is quite a ways from auto makers being able to rig markets or force customers to take what they want them to take. . . . There is no accounting for tastes, and tastes differ, and consumers are obviously exercising their rights to their own tastes. When it comes to dictating, the consumer is the dictator without peer.[6]

The *Phoenix Gazette* echoed this sentiment in its postmortem and, by implication, took a swipe at Vance Packard:

> Probably it is downright reactionary of us to suggest that industry still succeeds by producing what people want. But look at [the] Edsel and take one guess who's running things. It isn't Madison Avenue.

THE INDUSTRY HORSEPOWER BAN

Yet another timing-related factor that has been frequently cited was an industry ban on horsepower advertising. The 1958 Edsel was one of the most powerful cars on the market, and, as Pontiac would demonstrate in following years, a performance image is a very effective way to sell medium-priced cars. The Automobile Manufacturers Association (AMA), however, had just put a stop to the horsepower advertising "war" that had consumed the industry in the middle years of the decade. According to this line of thinking, the Edsel was thus denied one of its most powerful selling tools. Bunkie Knudsen, who ran Pontiac—which, after all, labored under the same restrictions—was upset about the AMA decision, too, but didn't let it stop him. As Knudsen showed, a performance image was as much a result of clever advertising and promotion as it was of horsepower claims per se.

OVER-RELIANCE ON MOTIVATIONAL RESEARCH

For years, one of the most popularly quoted—and widely believed—reasons for the failure of the Edsel was that the company had relied too heavily on motivational research. Motivational research was still in its infancy in the 1950s and, like any new field, was controversial. If a product connected with motivational research was a success, motivational research got at least some of the credit. If it was a flop, though, it was easy to blame the motivational research for everything.

In practice, of course, motivational research varies in quality. It can be good, bad, or indifferent. Obviously, a product decision based on bad motivational research is at risk. Within the auto industry, on the other hand, the common wisdom was that Ford Motor Company erred simply by using motivational research of any kind. The idea of hiring people—especially outside "experts" (a category of people then held in deep suspicion in Motown)—was an eye-opener at the time the Edsel was developed. This attitude seems laughably parochial today, but it was typical back then and accurately reflected the way product decisions were routinely made in Detroit.

After all, Henry Ford hadn't used any motivational research in developing the Model T. Nor had Edsel Ford consulted any outside research firms in conceptualizing the legendary Continental. As late as the 1970s, it was, simply put, the marketing intuition of a few key executives at each of the car companies that fueled high-stakes decisions on what to build and what not to build. A company fortunate enough to have a leader with intuitive marketing brilliance—such as Ford Motor Company prior to World War I or General Motors between the wars—soared ahead of its competitors. A company that didn't—such as Ford Motor Company between the wars or Chrysler Corporation in the 1940s—faltered. But, it was all, to a remarkable degree, hunches, guesswork, and luck.

Today tens of millions are routinely spent on the most elaborate kinds of marketing research before any new car hits the streets—even before approval is given to begin serious development work on it. The attitude in the industry has come full-circle and it is now considered suicidal not to use sophisticated market research of various types.

Of course, there are always pitfalls with any good thing. Research, even if astutely done, can only tell what people want at the time the research is conducted. It cannot tell the head of a car company with certainty what his customers will want three or four years down the road. Considering the lead times involved in developing new products, this remains a significant problem. It was, in fact, a problem with the Edsel to the extent that the market had changed dramatically between the time the motivational research was conducted in the winter of 1955–1956 and the time the Edsel appeared. As the respected *Louisville Times* remarked in its postmortem on the Edsel:

> We have an idea that old Henry, whose basic theory was simplicity ("any color as long as it's black") . . . might have got a wry chuckle out of this failure to win the approval of the consumers.
>
> Of course, old Henry's rigid theory was invalidated long ago when Ford began to lose money to competitors who did cater to the consumers. Perhaps the only valid theory is that consumers' tastes change and that not even the most modern methods of motivational research can forecast with confidence what those tastes will be.

Motivational research can also be put to both good and bad uses. S. I. Hayakawa, a noted semanticist and behavioral scientist who later became a U.S. Senator from California, attacked the Edsel after the fact in a well-circulated article entitled, "Why the Edsel Laid an Egg."[7] Hayakawa's main point—and a highly debatable, though popular, one—was that the Edsel had been deliberately designed (via motivational research) as a sexual fantasy device. Detroit cars, in general, were frequently seen in such terms in the 1950s, especially among intellectuals and others skeptical of big business (liberals, consumerists, etc.). Thus, the protruding bumper guards on Cadillacs were seen as female breasts, the long hoods and enormous hood ornaments on many brands were seen as phallic symbols, and so on.[8] There are still people who are convinced that the Edsel's "horse collar" grille was deliberately designed to resemble a very private part of the female anatomy and, therefore, provide subconscious sexual stimulation to male car buyers. The problem with this approach, continuing Hayakawa's reasoning, was that it failed to take into account cost/benefit relationships, or what Hayakawa called "the reality principle." Wrote Hayakawa:

> The trouble with selling symbolic gratification via such expensive items as . . . the Edsel Hermaphrodite . . . is the competition offered by much cheaper forms of symbolic gratification, such as *Playboy* (fifty cents a copy), *Astounding Science Fiction* (thirty-five cents a copy), and television (free).

Still, it is ironic to find Ford Motor Company faulted for recklessly engaging in and/or using motivational research. In the first place, most of the key decisions that drove the Edsel project were not, in fact, subjected to motivational research at all in any meaningful sense of that term. Critics such as Hayakawa notwithstanding, the styling, for example, was never subjected to critical evaluation outside the company. Neither was the all-important decision regarding the relative market positioning of the Edsel and the Mercury, nor was the high-risk decision to rely on an entirely new dealer network. Indeed, as noted in Chapter Seven, all of these decisions were either completed or well along toward completion before the controversial motivational research commenced.

The only areas upon which motivational research focused were in establishing the brand character of the Edsel and in selecting the name. In the case of the former, the motivational research revealed little of substance that had not been divined by Lincoln-Mercury product planners on their own as early as 1951, and it seems highly unlikely that the Edsel would have been very much different if no motivational research had taken place. In the case of the latter, the research was, indeed, extensive, but the results were never used because the name ultimately chosen had not been researched![9]

It is a simple fact that there were no critically important decisions made regarding the development of the Edsel that were significantly influenced by motivational research. Despite the hype churned out by the Edsel Division's public relations department, the Edsel was, in all important particulars, developed the same way cars had always been developed in Detroit: by the seat-of-the-pants intuition of those calling the shots.

THE STYLING

Even today, most people refer to the striking Edsel styling when they talk of the disaster, as if it died of the uglies. Jokes about the "horse collar" grille were certainly legion at the time, but this writer has never believed that styling was the major—or, even a significant—factor. In the first place, the original Edsel design was far from bad. Prepared by a talented team under the direction of Roy Brown, it had a high degree of unity and integrity to it—far more, in fact, than many "successful" cars of the era. Indeed, with the exception of the four-seater Thunderbird, the Edsel may have been the best-looking car built by Ford Motor Company that year. No less an authority than the former director of design at General Motors, the late David Holls, said of the 1958 Edsel:

> I thought it a very imaginative car, not laughable at all. It was controversial,
> brash. But, you couldn't run with the flock or you wouldn't have anything.[10]

Holls' point bears elaboration. The controversial nature of the Edsel styling, particularly the front-end styling, was deliberate. Brown wanted it to make a statement and stand out from the flock. He realized that such a design would be controversial—i.e., that a lot of people *wouldn't* like it—but that it didn't matter so long as enough people did. Another General Motors man, Mark Gjovik, the veteran advertising account executive at D'Arcy, Masius, Benton & Bowles (DMB&B), put the issue this way in a recent interview:

All successful products—regardless of the market they're in—need to have a distinct positioning to succeed. Without a strong identity in the consumer's mind, you don't really have much. All the truly successful brands stand for something that is quite distinctive. The essence of this is discrimination. To develop this distinct identity you are going to be saying "yes" in a big way to a segment of buyers, and "no" to a lot of others. But, to try to be all things to all people is really to end up being nothing to anybody.

Brown and his team of Edsel designers had the courage to stand for something. As a result, the 1958 Edsel bespoke an inner confidence about what it was trying to be, and there were (and are) many people quite favorably impressed with its looks. It was certainly far better styled than the more muted 1959 series. The 1959 lacked precisely the inner confidence the 1958 had in buckets; the 1959 looked as if it had been designed by the proverbial committee. ("Let's make it look like an Edsel without offending anyone.") As for the short-lived 1960 series, the less said about it the better. It was little more than a 1960 Ford with a 1959 Pontiac grille incongruously bolted onto the front. Obviously, even the committee had given up on it by that point.

THE NAME

It was long believed within Ford Motor Company that one of the key mistakes was the name. Hardly anyone—even at the time—thought "Edsel" was a brilliant choice. Despite the lengths to which car companies go in selecting names, though, it has never been convincingly established that a name really has much impact.

Some brands with horrendous names have been rather successful, indeed. Consider the two brands against which the Edsel was primarily targeted. "Buick" is not by any stretch a beautiful name, while "Oldsmobile" is about as hopeless as an automobile name can get. Think of "Fordmobile" or "Chryslermobile." Furthermore, companies invariably try to choose names that evoke youthful, dynamic, and glamorous connotations. Any name beginning with the word "old" would be ruled out of contention without a second thought. Yet, Oldsmobile was quite successful at the time and continued to be so for many decades.

On the other hand, superior names don't necessarily sell inferior products. When Chrysler was searching around for a way to breathe life into its moribund Windsor series in the early 1960s, it hit upon the stratagem of appropriating its most exciting designation: the 300. So, the dowdy Chrysler Windsor became the new Chrysler 300. Instead of the exciting name reinvigorating the dowdy car, however, the dowdy car devalued and ultimately killed the exciting name. The 300 was gone within a few seasons.

QUALITY CONTROL PROBLEMS WITH EARLY CARS

There is ample anecdotal evidence to support the charge that early Edsels were all-too-often quality control disasters. It is certainly true, of course, that any new car (especially in that era) was likely to have problems at first. This was true even of established brands undergoing the change-over to a new model. That was all the more reason Edsel quality should have been monitored with special care. Instead, it seems that cars were churned out as quickly as possible in order to get as many as possible to dealers by E-Day. The predictable result was that the most critical group of owners in terms of word-of-mouth advertising—the first ones to buy Edsels—had, in too many cases, absolutely dreadful experiences with them.

There were reports at the time that some of the key parts suppliers had experienced strikes during the critical start-up of production, which created shortages and, in some cases, last-minute tooling by new suppliers to produce the parts. In the haste to obtain and produce the needed pieces, tolerances were overlooked and quality suffered.

It has been alleged, as well, that early Edsels were deliberately sabotaged by workers in Ford and Mercury plants. This has never been proven and seems a stretch. It was true that in the B-O-P assembly plants, Pontiac, Olds, and Buick divisions all had personnel on site to maintain divisional quality standards. Neither McNamara (Ford) nor Reith (Mercury) permitted Edsel personnel in their plants.

Still, to believe that this was a general problem you would have to believe that Ford and Mercury workers were so fanatically protective of "their" brands that they would want to ruin a "rival" brand, even one produced by the same company. This sort of loyalty would have come as a surprise to veterans on both management and union sides at the time. Indeed, the absence of loyalty to particular companies—as evidenced, for example, by the chronically high turnover rate among employees of the assembly plants at all manufacturers—was, and remained, a major issue. The charge also ignores the fact that the Ford worker was now a Ford-Edsel worker. The Edsel brand was not an interloper; it was yet another company product being built in a Ford (or Mercury) plant. The worker had as much at stake in the success of the Edsel as in any other model or brand being built in the plant.

Mostly, it seems to this writer, the charge of sabotage in the assembly plants is evidence of the American obsession with conspiracies. Perhaps Larry Doyle —the man who built the Edsel dealer network and had as much riding on its success as anyone at Ford Motor Company—should be given the last word on the subject. After the Edsel was discontinued he responded this way:

Of course the Ford and Lincoln-Mercury Divisions didn't want to see another Ford company car in the field, but, as far as I know, anything they did at the executive and plant levels was in competitive good taste. On the other hand, at the distribution and dealer level, you got some rough infighting in terms of whispering and propaganda. If I'd been in one of the other divisions, I'd have done the same thing.[11]

TOO AMBITIOUS A PLAN

There were key figures within the company who thought the Crusoe-Reith plan for expansion in the medium-priced field, of which the Edsel was the most memorable component, was simply too ambitious. Among these figures were the chairman, Ernie Breech, and the sales vice-president, Jack Davis. Within a space of about two-and-a-half years, the company sought:

- To establish five separate automotive divisions. Thus, the company would expand from Ford, Lincoln-Mercury, and Continental to Ford, E-Car (Edsel), Mercury, Lincoln, and Continental.
- To establish five separate franchises, i.e., one for each new division.
- To launch a new nameplate (E-Car/Edsel) and reposition an old one (Mercury) at the same time.

In retrospect, the decision to have a stand-alone Continental Division seems loony. Even had the Continental Mark II met its sales projections, it is hard to see how a separate division could have been justified. The public always regarded it as a Lincoln, anyway.

As a practical matter, expanding the divisions as it was done required doubling the personnel at the divisional level, which made it difficult to find qualified people to fill all the slots. It was a terrific time for career advancement at the company, but, if anecdotal evidence is to be believed, it played havoc with efficiency.

When James Nance was given the unhappy task of consolidating the Mercury and Lincoln divisions in 1957, the net savings to the company amounted to $80 million per year in overhead. To put it another way, having the separate divisions had added more than $250 to the cost of each Mercury and Lincoln sold in 1957. In 1958, that figure would have risen to more than $400 per car. And, this was after Continental Division had already been folded into Lincoln. The added cost might have made sense for the Edsel, which was trying to establish its own identity and was supposed to be a high-volume brand, but it was questionable for Lincoln and downright silly for the Continental.[12]

Secondly, the heart of the Crusoe-Reith plan was the need to expand Ford's dealer body—and, with it, the company's sales and marketing muscle—from 8,000 dealers to something closer to the 16,500 that General Motors had. Crusoe and Reith reasoned that this was impossible with two franchises (Ford and Lincoln-Mercury). While they were probably correct, it did not automatically follow that five separate franchises were a viable idea all at once. In general, there was little thought given to gradually growing into the new, larger company Crusoe and Reith had in mind. It was supposed to happen—poof!—all at once. This obsession with instant results may have been the pervasive underlying flaw of the Crusoe-Reith strategy.

Finally, it seems to this writer at any rate, that the market positioning of the Edsel and the Mercury may have been the single worst feature of the Crusoe-Reith plan and warrants being discussed as a separate issue here.

THE MARKET POSITIONING

What Ford Motor Company needed was another medium-priced car to supplement the Mercury, which had achieved a fairly successful presence in the lower end of the market against Dodge and Pontiac. The company had nothing in the Buick/Chrysler class. So, with the lower half of the medium-priced market successfully covered, what was needed was a Buick/Chrysler equivalent. Obviously. All of the plans prior to the Crusoe-Reith plan put this new car (the Monterey, the E-Car, etc.) into the open slot between Mercury and Lincoln. The Crusoe-Reith plan reversed this.

As Crusoe and Reith conceived it, the Edsel was pegged to compete in the traditional Mercury market, which meant the Mercury had to be moved up into the Buick/Chrysler class. That, as a practical matter, meant that the company had to establish from scratch not one, but two new medium-priced lines. The traditional Mercury buyer wasn't going to buy the new Mercury—it was now too expensive—and the Edsel was a totally unknown quantity. In effect, the company was throwing away two decades of work in the lower end of the medium-priced field and starting all over again.

In fact, the Mercury never moved as far upscale—or surrendered as much of its traditional market—as it was supposed to. It did not do so because the Crusoe-Reith plan for Mercury and Lincoln to share a common body was wrecked by MacPherson's decision to have the 1958 Lincoln switch over to unibody construction. The Mercury was moved up to a certain extent, but not enough to leave a meaningful gap for the Edsel. At the same time, Ford was squeezing the Edsel from the other end of the spectrum with the Fairlane 500 series. In 1958, the lowest-priced Mercury four-door sedan carried a suggested retail price of $2,617, while the top-end Ford four-door listed for $2,499. That left a price gap of $118. It was a squeeze play the Edsel could ill afford. In the end, the overall price spread of the Edsel ($2,519–$3,801) was hardly different from that of the Mercury ($2,547–$4,118), and the Edsel was left struggling to plug a price gap that didn't exist.

THE SEPARATE DEALER NETWORK

Ford Motor Company was determined to launch the Edsel with a separate dealer network. In doing so, it was doubling the odds against success. It was attempting not only to establish a new brand, but a new dealer in every community, as well. When Ford Motor Company had introduced the original Mercury in 1939, it simply added it to the Ford-Lincoln franchise. After the war, Lincoln and Mercury were split off from Ford. There was no compelling reason why the Edsel could not have been run through the established national network of Ford or Lincoln-Mercury dealers.

The contribution of the local dealer is something chronically underestimated in Detroit. The tendency over the years has been to treat dealers as necessary evils, as a bunch of low-life hucksters who are taking a free ride on the manufacturer's brilliance—not as valued allies who pull their fair share of the load. This view was certainly an element in the company's thinking. True, the company recognized it needed more good dealers to act as sales outlets, and that was a key motivator for the Edsel program. True, too, general manager Krafve was on record as wanting top-quality dealers who could service the Edsel in a quality manner. Too little thought was given, however, to the difficulty in establishing those good dealers or in the vital contribution good dealers could make in putting the brand over. The company thought its reputation and the $50 million spent in promotion was all that was required— i.e., that the promotional efforts of the dealers themselves would be more-or-less irrelevant.

Yet, a good dealer has an established customer base that may have little to do with the efforts of the manufacturer. Consider: Why does a man buy, say, a Dodge? It might be because he shops all around and buys the best car he can in his price class and, in his considered opinion, that car is a Dodge. Or, it might be that he is a Dodge buyer, someone who is—for whatever reason— unswervingly loyal to Dodge. Or, it might be loyalty to a particular dealer, a factor rarely given serious thought in Detroit. Possibly the Dodge agency is the only one in his price class convenient to him. Perhaps the man would really prefer a Pontiac, but the Pontiac dealer is unacceptable for geographic or other reasons. Perhaps the Dodge dealer has always given him great service.

Perhaps his buddy (or brother-in-law, or lodge brother, or whomever) works for the Dodge agency. Perhaps the Dodge agency is simply the most aggressive and effective local dealer in the man's price bracket. In short, there are any number of reasons that this man might buy a Dodge that have little or nothing to do with the inherent virtues of the Dodge car and a lot to do with where it is sold and who is selling it.

The above is particularly important given the public's attitude that the cars in any given price class are roughly comparable, at least in a functional sense. Alfred Sloan had noted this in the 1920s (see Chapter Three). That is why General Motors expended so much energy developing price points and superficial elements such as styling. Later on, this approach was codified by advertising agencies under the anagram "USP," which stands for "Unique Selling Proposition" and refers to something that a given brand has that the competition does not.

In order to be appealing, a product needs at least one USP—and the more the better. A USP doesn't necessarily have to be *objectively* important, though, so long as it can be made to *seem* important. This is why detergent boxes in the grocery stores all say "new," "improved," "contains special whiteness ingredient #F38," and so on. These are USPs. The Edsel, entering a furiously competitive market without an established customer base and without established dealers who had their own customer bases, desperately needed USPs. The front-end styling was arguably one (assuming a prospect liked it) and the push-button transmission mounted on the steering wheel hub was certainly another. The three-stage dual-thermostat cooling system was yet another, although it was probably too esoteric for most customers. Ditto for the self-adjusting brakes. That, however, was about it. If the Edsel had been offered through existing Ford dealers (who had their own established customers), the dearth of USPs would not have mattered so much. Considering that it was intended to sell through start-up dealers, though, the Edsel's lack of uniqueness was a major failing. To once again quote publicist Gayle Warnock: "When they find out it's got four wheels and one engine, just like the next car, they're liable to be disappointed."[13] Many of them were.

In any case, it was a whole lot harder establishing a solid network of Edsel dealers than anyone at the company expected. Sadly, when the Edsel failed to meet its sales targets, it was the dealers who suffered the most. Few of them were able to attain profitability, and many were forced to switch to other brands in order to survive, or to go out of business altogether. Many were personally wiped out. Needless-to-say, scores of dead Edsel dealerships dotting the landscape did absolutely nothing to advance the brand's reputation with the general public. Once a brand gets tagged as a "loser," it becomes extraordinarily difficult to get people to invest their purchasing dollars in it.

MANAGEMENT'S OVER-EXPECTATIONS

It is an article of faith that the Edsel was a flop—but, was it? By what standard? Ford officials wanted to sell a minimum of 100,000 units the first year, with 200,000 being the hope. Instead, they sold 60,000 and, based on early sales reports, had written off the whole three-year effort almost before the 1958 model year had begun. The 1959 and 1960 models were dead letters in Dearborn before they ever hit the streets.

As has been noted, however, the 100,000/200,000 sales range was based on the market as it existed in 1955 when the Edsel program was officially launched. In terms of market share, that translated into 3.3 percent to 6.7 percent of the medium-priced segment. By the time the Edsel appeared, of course, that segment had contracted by 60 percent. The Edsel still sold 60,000 units, or about 5 percent of the medium-priced cars registered that year. This was almost identical to the market segment penetration the Mercury had achieved in 1939 in its maiden year.

So, by what standard was the 1958 Edsel a failure? In terms of market penetration, it fell solidly within the range of what it was supposed to do and can hardly be faulted for the general, temporary deterioration in the market. By the mid-1960s, the medium-priced market had largely recovered, but, instead of hanging in there, company management threw in the towel. The Edsel line was drastically pared back for 1959 (with the big, Mercury-based models scrubbed at the last minute) and barely alive and certainly no competition for anybody by 1960. Ironically, the Edsel Comet—subsequently produced as a Mercury—was one of the big success stories of the 1960 model year.

There are more than a few industry observers who remain convinced that the Edsel would have made it if the company had just hung in there. Instead, Ford Motor Company turned a potential silk purse into a certain sow's ear and let it go down in the record books as the greatest automotive marketing disaster of all time. Persistence would have involved risk and some pain, but hardly more pain than that caused by the actual fiasco.

The real failure in the Edsel saga had little to do with the car. It was a failure of Ford Motor Company management on almost too many levels to count. The greatest of these failures, however, may have been the inability to realize that the 1958 Edsel was actually a modest success that deserved continued support.

BONSALL'S 20/20 HINDSIGHT SOLUTION

In view of all the factors discussed above, it seems possible that the Edsel could have worked well had it been conceived and marketed along the following lines:

- It should have been positioned to fill the obvious gap that existed between Mercury and Lincoln.

- It should have been sold through existing Ford Motor Company dealers. If it had been positioned between Mercury and Lincoln in the Buick/Chrysler segment, it would have been a logical companion line for the powerful Ford dealer body. With the four-seater Thunderbird, Ford dealers were to prove that they could sell fairly expensive products and this would have given the company two strong franchises: Ford-Edsel and Lincoln-Mercury. After the Edsel was established, it could easily have been split off, much as Mercury and Lincoln were split off from Ford in the late 1940s.

- Quality should have been fanatically monitored, particularly with the first cars off the line. These were the ones that, for good or ill, would establish the Edsel's all-important word-of-mouth reputation.

- There was nothing inherently wrong with having a separate Edsel Division. Indeed, considering the successful General Motors example, it made a lot of sense, and rendered it that much easier to establish the Edsel as a separate brand in the public's mind.

- The commitment, however, should have been long-term. If anecdotal evidence is correct, the plug was pulled on the Edsel before the first car was sold! Even by the most generous accounts, the decision was made in the first few months following E-Day. In contrast, it took years to establish the Mercury brand. If Ford Motor Company management wasn't willing to invest several years of effort in the Edsel, they didn't *deserve* to succeed.

- They also had a helluva nerve suckering dealers and customers into investing serious money in a brand into which they were unwilling to make a long-term commitment themselves. It is a fact that most Edsel buyers—and, some would contend all Edsel buyers—bought a brand that Ford Motor Company knew was going to be discontinued. Considering the well-known resale value penalty attached to "orphan" brands, this constituted bad faith on a grand scale.

Epilogue

Richard E. Krafve left Ford Motor Company even before the demise of the car he had helped to launch. At the time of the official obituaries, he was vice-president of Raytheon and later rose to president. "You put your heart and your guts into a thing like that," he was quoted as saying when he heard the news. "If only the timing had been different."[1]

Roy Brown was sent to Ford of Great Britain. There, he directed the design of the highly successful Cortina, the car that put the company back on the map in Europe. By the 1970s, he had returned to Detroit and was in charge of the exteriors studio responsible for Ford intermediates, standard-size cars, and the Thunderbird. Fourteen years after the launch of the Edsel, he was unrepentant:

> I still believe it was a well-designed car. . . . At least on the '58, trying to find a bad line on that car is a difficult job. It has real nice lines, all the detailing is good, and so forth. So, I [am] just as pleased today, after some fourteen years, as I was when we first did it.[2]

Gayle Warnock left the company for a time to go to work for ITT, but was brought back to manage the launch of the Mercury Cougar in 1966 (as a 1967 model). "That way you can bat .500," a friend at Lincoln-Mercury Division chided him. After the Cougar, he was named public affairs director for the company's Philco subsidiary. He, too, continued to defend the Edsel:

> As a concept, I think there was nothing wrong with the Edsel. Virtually everything about the design—everything including the so-called horse-collar grille—has appeared since on some other car, although I must say Pontiac did possibly a little better job, but, then, that was ten years later.[3]

After Mercury Division was yanked out from under him, Jack Reith was transferred to a job at the corporate level where he could mark enough time to qualify for his bonuses. After that, he left for a job with Crosley in Cincinnati. Shortly thereafter, he died of a self-inflicted gunshot wound. His friends believed it was accidental.

Emmet Judge went to Lincoln and Mercury Division (later the M-E-L Division) when Nance took over. After the big "Reith" Mercury died in 1960, he went to Westinghouse in an executive capacity, then did private consulting work.

After a tumultuous career in the auto industry, James J. Nance decided to get out of cars for good. He subsequently built a respected and successful career in Cleveland banking circles. As he noted in an interview in the 1970s:

> I welcomed the opportunity to run a bank. You can't do anything without money. Sooner or later everybody ends up at the bank.[4]

Jack Davis, Ford Motor Company's veteran sales chief, left the company when McNamara rose to prominence and bought a hotel in Petoskey, Michigan, in the Traverse Bay resort area in the western part of the state. He made a great success of it.

Richard Stout enjoyed a varied career that included stints with the General Motors Styling Section as a designer (1947–50), with Lincoln-Mercury as a product planner (1950–53), with Packard as a designer (1953–56), with Edsel Division as a product planner (November, 1956, until January, 1957), then with Ford corporate product planning under Nance until the fall of 1957, and, finally, with M-E-L (1957–60) and Lincoln-Mercury (1962–66).

○

Robert McNamara went on to assume the presidency of Ford Motor Company in 1960. His personal triumph was the Ford Falcon, which an associate described as being just like McNamara: "He wore granny glasses and he built a granny car." Another one of McNamara's associates in the Ford days summed up his career with the company this way: "He was the best thing that ever happened to Ford Motor Company. His leaving was the second best thing."[5]

Following the election of John F. Kennedy in 1960, McNamara was named Secretary of Defense. How and why this came about is still a subject of some speculation. One story is that, following the power play McNamara had exercised in 1958 in getting rid of Jim Nance, the Ford family became fearful of losing control of the family business to the Whiz Kids. (In the face of McNamara's intense ambition, this was not necessarily an unreasonable fear, either.)[6] Eleanor Clay Ford, the matriarch, was said to be especially hostile to McNamara, and it was well-known in Dearborn that no important executive decision was ever made without her tacit approval. Dick Stout recalled the scenario this way:

> Mrs. Ford was the force, apparently, behind the move to get rid of McNamara. Once he got into power it became evident that they were going to have to get rid of him somehow. [Henry Ford II] offered to clean up the debts [of the Kennedy campaign] on the condition that they would take McNamara off his hands. Then, McNamara would become Secretary of the Treasury.[7]

It is known that McNamara was first offered the Treasury post, although he ended up as Secretary of Defense. In that position, he managed the build-up of America's involvement in the Vietnamese War, and brought his obsession with statistical analysis to bear in various ways with the military.[8] The most notable example was the F-111 fighter plane, which he insisted—over heated objections from the military chiefs—be developed as a universal aircraft to serve the needs of all branches of the service. Having one plane suited his bean counter mind, but the F-111 was a failure and quickly became known as the "Flying Edsel." In 1967, President Johnson packed McNamara off to head the World Bank.

Rich Thomas, the economics editor of *Newsweek* magazine at the time this book was written, grew up in Detroit and followed McNamara's career for more than thirty years. Thomas dismisses the achievements of Whiz Kids, in general, even including their celebrated instituting of cost controls and statistical systems at Ford Motor Company after the war. "Any competent accountant" could have done as much, Thomas asserts. As for McNamara himself, Thomas notes: "There are people who go from failure to failure and rise."[9]

○

Foote, Cone & Belding, the original Edsel advertising agency, took a bath on its association. According to press reports at the time, it had spent as much as $1,000,000 through its Detroit office before the first Edsel billings came through. Then, it was unceremoniously dumped from the account at the start of the 1959 model year. It is certain the agency never made a dime for all its troubles. Its reputation was also severely tarnished. Five years after the launch, when Tim Howley, the noted automotive writer, went to work for the agency, people were still walking around in a state of shock. Nevertheless, FC&B retained important accounts, such as General Foods, Lever Brothers, and Trans World Airways (TWA). FC&B was bloodied, but survived.

○

It's an ill wind, indeed, that doesn't blow somebody some good. When General Motors' Saturn Corporation subsidiary was in the planning stages, Skip LeFauve, the president/CEO, bought a case of Gale Warnock's memoirs, *The Edsel Affair*, and gave a copy to all his executives. He insisted they read it and underline everything Ford did wrong with the Edsel. Curiously, LeFauve managed to take one of Ford's biggest blunders—the dedicated dealer network—and, by fanatical attention to customer service, make it one of Saturn's strongest selling points.

○

Following the debacle, Ford Motor Company went on to record extraordinary successes. Ironically, the Edsel may have helped make those successes possible. The increased manufacturing and assembly capacity the company developed for the Edsel was a godsend when it was needed in the early 1960s. The Ford Falcon—which was a huge hit, selling over 400,000 cars during the 1960 model year and becoming the best-seller among the Big Three compacts—might not otherwise have been possible on that scale, certainly not as early as 1960. The same goes for the Ford Mustang—introduced in April, 1964, as a 1965 model—which proved an even bigger success, outselling even the Falcon in its debut model run. Moreover, the extra capacity was bought at 1956–57 prices, providing additional savings over what it would have cost in the

1960s. Taking a long-term view, it is even possible to say that the Edsel program (if not the Edsel car itself) may have ended up producing a sizable profit for the company.

As for the Lincoln, it finally found its market, beginning with the celebrated 1961 series "slab-sided" Continental sedans. The Mark III, introduced in 1968, continued Lincoln's upward momentum. By the mid-1990s, Lincoln had achieved parity with Cadillac in the luxury automobile field.

The shortcomings in the medium-priced field that had led to the development of the Edsel continued to dog the company, however. With only three brands and two dealer networks, it proved impossible to expand corporate market share much beyond the 25–30 percent range. The company was, thus, consigned to permanent status as America's second auto producer, although a vibrant second capable of thriving in the brutally competitive automobile industry.

In retrospect, it seems that the Edsel really was the company's best chance to challenge General Motors for supremacy. Given the decline of the latter in the 1980s and 1990s, and the successes of Ford Motor Company with breakthrough models such as the Taurus, the presence of a second medium-priced line might well have enabled the company to realize its dream of recapturing the premier position in the industry.

Notes

CHAPTER ONE. EDSEL FORD: THE EARLY YEARS

The most important resources drawn upon in the writing of this chapter include Allan Nevins, *Ford: The Times, the Man, the Company*, Nevins and Hills, *Ford: Expansion and Challenge, 1915–1932*, Charles Sorensen, *My Forty Years with Ford*, and the author's collection of Ford and Lincoln-related material. Hugo Pfau, *The Custom Body Era*, provided important insights into Edsel Ford's management style at Lincoln. The Ford Archives at the Henry Ford Museum in Dearborn also supplied significant material.

1. Ford Motor Company papers, author's collection.

2. Edsel, age ten, reportedly assisted his father in building the famous "Old 999" race car.

3. In the end, the court ruled that the agreement to compensate Lincoln's stockholders had, in fact, existed, but said it was unenforcable because it violated Michigan law.

4. In June, 1924, Henry Ford gave $25,000 to the Y.M.C.A. At the time, it was described by the newspapers as the first gift he had ever made to an organized charity. He was, by then, a billionaire.

5. *Automobile Quarterly*, May, 1991, p. 26.

6. Forbes and Foster, pp. 105–106.

7. Ford Motor Company papers, author's collection.

CHAPTER TWO. EDSEL FORD: THE FINAL YEARS

The most important resources drawn upon in the writing of this chapter include Allan Nevins, *Ford: The Times, the Man, the Company*, Nevins and Hills, *Ford: Expansion and Challenge, 1915–1932*, Charles Sorensen's, *My Forty Years with Ford*, and the author's collection of Ford and Lincoln-related material. Harry Bennett, *We Never Called Him Henry*, provided insights into the inner workings of Ford, the man and the company. An interview with E. T. Gregorie offered insights into Edsel Ford's involvement with design. The Ford Archives at the Henry Ford Museum in Dearborn also supplied significant material.

1. *Special-Interest Autos*, Jul–Aug, 1971, p. 46.
2. Ibid., p. 18.
3. Ibid., pp. 15–21.
4. Sorensen, pp. 256–257.
5. *Special-Interest Autos*, Jul–Aug, 1974, p. 16.
6. Ibid., p. 16.
7. Ford Motor Company papers, author's collection.
8. The Ford roof stampings were shared on the first Mercurys.
9. *Special-Interest Autos*, Jul–Aug, 1974, pp. 19–20.
10. One line of thought contends that the six-cylinder engine was developed as a military project in order to secure government contracts, then used in the cars as an afterthought. This may be true. It may also be true that the military project was a convenient ruse to develop an engine for the Ford car that could be developed in no other way. It was not easy getting things done at Ford Motor Company in the 1930s and early 1940s! The secrecy and indirection were so compulsive that it was often hard even for the participants to tell what was going on—or why.
11. Ford Motor Company papers, author's collection.
12. Conde interview, author's collection.
13. Bennett, p. 168.
14. In terms of buying power, $40,000 then was worth around $1 million today.

CHAPTER THREE. DEVELOPMENT OF THE MARKET

The most important resources drawn upon in the writing of this chapter include Alfred Sloan, *My Years With General Motors*, Walter Chrysler, *Life of an American Workman*, and Forbes and Foster, *Automotive Giants of America*. General Motors papers in the author's collection also provided significant material.

1. Ford Motor Company papers, author's collection.
2. Chrysler, p. 143.
3. Sloan, pp. 58–70.
4. Ibid., pp. 58–70.
5. Forbes and Foster, p. 240.
6. Ibid., p. 240–241.
7. Sloan, p. 155.
8. Yes, complete with the pretentious English spelling.

CHAPTER FOUR. PROLOGUE TO THE EDSEL

The most important resources drawn upon in the writing of this chapter include Allan Nevins and Frank E. Hill, *Ford: Decline and Rebirth, 1933–1962*, and Richard Stout,

Make 'Em Shout Hooray! The Ford Archives at the Henry Ford Museum in Dearborn also supplied significant research material.

1. Borg-Warner automatic transmissions were supplied for Ford and Mercury, while Lincoln used the GM Hydra-Matic.

2. Stout, p. 96.

3. This was before the Army and the Air Force became separate service branches.

4. The "solution" then is generally to call in another group of bean counters, who show flashy results at first but then continue the deterioration until yet another group of bean counters is tapped. General Motors has been undergoing this slow torture for forty years, during which time its market share has been almost halved. Some would contend Ford has, too.

5. Stout, p. 106. "What is the purpose of a gray-iron foundry?" This was a favorite question of the Whiz Kids, one that they delighted in asking of the unsuspecting. To make castings, might come the tentative reply. "To make money!" the Whiz Kids would shout, then dissolve into laughter.

6. Stout interview, author's collection.

7. According to Richard Stout, who was in Lincoln-Mercury product planning at the time, in an interview with the author, the staff at the General Motors Proving Ground was convinced that Ford, Mercury, and Lincoln shared a common body. To have a laugh at Ford Motor Company's expense, they planned a little show in which the front door of a Lincoln would be removed and bolted onto a Ford. It wasn't until they actually tried to do it that they discovered the Lincoln body was different.

8. Stout, p. 109.

CHAPTER FIVE. LEARNING THEIR ABCs

The most important resources drawn upon in the writing of this chapter include Richard Stout, *Make 'Em Shout Hooray!*, and several interviews with Stout. The Ford Archives at the Henry Ford Museum in Dearborn also supplied significant material.

1. This was a problem that General Motors would confront again—with a vengeance—in the 1980s.

2. Young and Quinn, p. 86.

3. One might speculate as to the reasons Ford and Chrysler were so slow on the uptake. Chrysler was an "engineer's" company, where, in terms of product development, the engineering staff reigned supreme in the 1930s and 1940s. Thus, the 1934 Chrysler Airflow was revolutionary from an engineering standpoint—and in the truest meaning of that much abused term. It was generally accepted by industry observers, though, that what killed the Airflow in the marketplace was poor styling. Even so, the debacle didn't loosen the engineers' grip on product development, and it wasn't until 1949 that Chrysler hired Virgil Exner and began to develop an independent design staff worthy of the name. Under Exner—who was a GM alumnus—in-

terchangeability at Chrysler became much more sophisticated in a hurry. At Ford, the problem was most likely the obsessively centralized management style of Henry Ford. Until his forced retirement in 1945, there were no well-developed marketing, engineering, or styling staffs and, therefore, no one on the payroll whose job it was to think about things such as the GM interchangeability program. Again, it was a GM alumnus, Richard Stout, who spread the word.

4. The Olds 98 shared the B-body. The Olds 76 and 88 lines used the smaller A-body in common with Chevrolet and Pontiac.

5. Even General Motors wasn't infallible, though. The replacement for the A-body proved too costly for Chevy and Pontiac. It was then redesignated the BO-body and foisted off onto Buick and Olds (hence the "BO" designation). Although these designations were intended for internal consumption only—i.e., General Motors never referred to bodies by letter designation with the general public—people within the company found "BO" amusing, to say the least, so it was switched to "OB." Olds dropped the B-body after 1951 and used only the OB-body in 1952–53, while Buick used it for the low-buck Special. In 1959, General Motors went hell-for-leather for interchangeability when every car line from Chevy through Cadillac was built off the same B-body.

6. Stout, p. 109.

7. Stout interview, author's collection.

8. Stout, p. 113.

9. Ibid., p. 113.

10. Ibid., p. 115.

11. Ford Motor Company papers, author's collection.

CHAPTER SIX. THE PLOT THICKENS

The most important resources drawn upon in the writing of this chapter include Allan Nevins and Frank E. Hill, *Ford: Decline and Rebirth, 1933–1962*, John Brooks, *Fate of the Edsel and Other Business Adventures*, Richard Stout, *Make 'Em Shout Hooray!*, and several interviews with Stout. Interviews with Roy Brown, Jr., Bob Jones, Gary Griffiths, and other Edsel designers were invaluable in tracing the design evolution of the Edsel. Ford Motor Company papers in the author's collection also supplied significant material.

1. In an interview with the author, Richard Stout recalled that the Continental Division and the Special Products (E-Car) were actually established as early as the spring of 1953. Special Products was then under Krafve—but still a quasi-subsidiary of Lincoln-Mercury Division—who continued with his Lincoln-Mercury duties in tandem. If so, Krafve couldn't have had much to do for two years with the Special Products side. Recalled Stout: "Special Products was created in the spring of 1953. I knew as I went to Packard in June, 1953, and was sorry I could not be part of the new group. Wish I could help fill in what happened between 1953–55!"

2. Ford Motor Company papers, author's collection.

3. Ibid.

4. Ibid.

5. This was standard practice in the industry. A core model would be selected and the design would be made using that series and body style. All other models would then be derived from it. The core model for the 1958 Edsel line seems to have been the Pacer convertible. If so, it was one of the few times a low-volume model, such as a convertible, was chosen for that role.

6. Ford Motor Company papers, author's collection.

7. *Special-Interest Autos*, Nov–Dec, 1973, p. 14.

8. Ford Motor Company papers, author's collection.

CHAPTER SEVEN. MOTIVATIONAL RESEARCH

The most important resources drawn upon in the writing of this chapter include John Brooks, *Fate of the Edsel and Other Business Adventures*, Richard Stout, *Make 'Em Shout Hooray!*, and several interviews with Stout. Ford Motor Company papers in the author's collection also supplied significant material.

1. Brooks, p. 27.

2. Ibid., pp. 29–30. "By looking at those respondents whose annual incomes range from $4,000 to $11,000," the report read, "we can make an . . . observation. A considerable percentage of these respondents are in the 'somewhat' category on ability to mix cocktails. Evidently, they do not have much confidence in their cocktail-mixing ability. We may infer that these respondents are aware of the fact that they are in the learning process. They may be able to mix Martinis or Manhattans, but beyond these popular drinks they don't have much of a repertoire."

3. Ibid., p. 32.

4. Ford Motor Company papers, author's collection.

5. Ibid.

6. Brooks, p. 34.

7. Ibid., p. 35.

8. Ford Motor Company papers, author's collection.

9. Ibid. As a postscript to the entire episode, Wallace felt he owed Miss Moore an explanation:

Because you were so kind to us in our early and hopeful days of looking for a suitable name, I feel a deep obligation to report on the events that have ensued. And I feel I must do so before the public announcement of same, come November 19.

We have chosen a name out of the more than six-thousand-odd candidates that we gathered. It has a certain ring to it. An air of gaiety and zest. At least, that's what we keep saying. Our name, dear Miss Moore, is—"Edsel."

I know you will share your sympathies with us.

A few days later, Moore replied:

> I thank you for the letter just received from you, of November 8th. You
> have the certainly ideal thing—with the Ford identity ingeniously sym-
> bolized. (I am a little piqued that I concentrated on physical phenomena.)
> At all events, thank you for informing me of the Company's choice—a
> matter of keen interest. Am quite partisan. I do wish the Company designs
> to "lead."
>
> Mr. Young is possessed of esprit and I hope is thriving.

CHAPTER EIGHT. THE SHOW OPENS

The most important resources drawn upon in the writing of this chapter include John
Brooks, *Fate of the Edsel and Other Business Adventures*, Richard Stout, *Make 'Em Shout
Hooray!*, and several interviews with Stout. Ford Motor Company papers in the au-
thor's collection also supplied significant material.

1. Brooks, p. 38.
2. Ibid., p. 39
3. Ford Motor Company papers, author's collection.
4. *Special-Interest Autos*, Nov–Dec, 1973, p. 12.
5. In an interview with the author Richard Stout recalled: "These were fun shows;
Emmet was very good at this."
6. Brooks, p. 46
7. Ibid., p. 48.
8. Ford Motor Company papers, author's collection.

CHAPTER NINE. FIRST TRAGEDY . . .

The most important resources drawn upon in the writing of this chapter include John
Brooks, *Fate of the Edsel and Other Business Adventures*, Richard Stout, *Make 'Em Shout
Hooray!*, and several interviews with Stout. Ford Motor Company papers in the au-
thor's collection also supplied significant material.

1. In recent years, methods have been developed to build both unibody and body-
and-frame cars on the same line. It was not thought possible when the Wixom facility was planned.
2. Significantly, Chrysler, which was then planning to switch its entire fleet over
to unibody construction by 1960, did not attempt to use it for its Imperial line. The
Imperial was roughly equivalent in size and purpose to the Lincoln.
3. For a detailed analysis of the decline of Studebaker-Packard, see *More Than
They Promised, The Studebaker Story*, also published by Stanford University Press. It
has been well documented, too, that Nance tried to buy bodies from Ford Motor
Company to supplement or replace those at Studebaker-Packard. Recalled Richard
Stout, who was still with Studebaker-Packard at this point: "I made detailed draw-

ings—Packard with Lincoln body, Clipper with Mercury body, Studebaker with Ford body." According to some sources, Ford Motor Company even agreed to sell the Lincoln tooling—presumably after Lincoln was done with it at the close of the 1957 model run—but nothing came of it in the end.

4. It is not clear if Reith was included in the group at this point.

5. Yes, corporate. Ford Motor Company, the last of the privately held major auto manufacturers, had gone public in 1956.

6. Stout interview, author's collection.

7. Stout, p. 187.

8. It was, in fact, Lincoln and Mercury Division—unhyphenated, as if to preserve at least a shadow of the separation between the two brands. Continental Division had already been folded into Lincoln Division.

9. *Car Life*, March, 1958, p. 61.

10. Ibid., p. 61.

11. Ford Motor Company papers, author's collection.

12. Ford, Edsel, Mercury, Lincoln, and Continental Divisions were then in existence and separate bodies were used to build Ford, Ford Thunderbird, Mercury, Lincoln, and Continental cars.

13. Brooks, p. 62.

14. *Motor Trend*, October, 1957, p. 25.

15. So, too, was the fact that the article was buried at the back of the issue, on pages 62–63 of an 82-page magazine. The bloom was clearly off the Edsel publicity rose.

16. *Motor Trend*, December, 1957, pp. 62–63.

17. Ibid., pp. 62–63.

18. Ibid., pp. 62–63.

19. Ford Motor Company papers, author's collection.

20. Brooks, pp. 57–58. *Consumer Reports'* attitude toward cars, in general, can perhaps best be divined by its conclusion on the 1959 Cadillac Sixty Special in its 1959 new car issue: "An expenditure sufficient to buy this Cadillac will also buy two other very satisfactory U.S. vehicles, which would provide more, and more various, services to facilitate a family's motoring pleasure." If Edsel's David Wallace didn't know why someone would pay $6,000 for a Cadillac, either, he, at least, took the trouble to try and find out (see Chapter Seven). *Consumer Reports*, apparently, didn't know and didn't care. Cars were only appliances to them.

21. Ibid., pp. 57–58.

22. *Car Life*, October, 1957, p. 27.

23. Ibid., March, 1958, p. 62.

24. Ibid., p. 62.

CHAPTER TEN. . . . THEN FARCE

The most important resources drawn upon in the writing of this chapter include John Brooks, *Fate of the Edsel and Other Business Adventures*, Richard Stout, *Make 'Em Shout*

Hooray!, and several interviews with Stout. Interviews with Roy Brown, Jr., Bob Jones, Gary Griffiths, and other Edsel designers were invaluable in tracing the design evolution of the Edsel. Ford Motor Company papers in the author's collection also supplied significant material.

1. Ford Motor Company papers, author's collection.

2. Brooks, p. 66.

3. Ibid., p. 64.

4. This must have been especially traumatic for Nance considering he had gone through a similar experience two years earlier with Studebaker-Packard. There is only but so much a man can take.

5. Ford Motor Company papers, author's collection.

6. Ibid. Considering the source—a car company press release—this historical data is remarkably accurate. Some of the years are off slightly, but the only gross error is the "Willys-American." First, it was the Americar and, second, it was only a series in the Willys range. Launched in 1940 as a replacement for the successful Willys 77, the Americar was modestly successful until World War II halted production. After the war, Willys made a high-risk decision to concentrate its efforts on the legendary Jeep. The decision paid off and the Willys nameplate was very much alive and well when this press release was issued, although it was eventually dropped in favor of the Kaiser nameplate, when they became Kaiser Jeeps. Henry Kaiser had bought the company in 1953. Later it was sold to American Motors and, still later, to Chrysler Corporation.

7. Brooks, p. 66.

8. Stout interview, author's collection.

CHAPTER ELEVEN. FINAL ACT . . . AND CURTAIN

The most important resources drawn upon in the writing of this chapter include John Brooks, *Fate of the Edsel and Other Business Adventures*, Richard Stout, *Make 'Em Shout Hooray!*, and several interviews with Stout. Interviews with Bob Jones and other Edsel designers were invaluable in tracing the design evolution of the Edsel. An interview with Charles Jordan, former vice-president of design at General Motors, was invaluable in understanding the 1959 GM styling program. Ford Motor Company, General Motors, and Chrysler Corporation papers in the author's collection also supplied significant material.

1. General Motors papers, author's collection.

2. This story speaks volumes about the way in which critical design decisions were often made in Detroit in this era.

3. *Automotive Industries*, October 15, 1959, p. 32.

4. Brooks, p. 67.

5. Ford Motor Company papers, author's collection.

6. Ibid.

The most important resources drawn upon in the writing of this chapter include Ford Motor Company papers in the author's collection and interviews with David Holls, Richard Stout and Rich Thomas.

1. This and all following quotations in this chapter were taken from Ford Motor Company papers in the author's collection unless otherwise noted.

2. Brooks, p. 67.

3. Ibid., p. 22.

4. *Motor Trend*, October, 1957, p. 8.

5. Brooks, p. 70.

6. Ibid., pp. 68–69.

7. Hayakawa, p. 62. As a Senator, Hayakawa became famous for sleeping through Senate debates—which, after all, is the only rational response to such interminable semantic nonsense—and earned the author's undying admiration for his argument against returning the Panama Canal to Panama. With unassailable logic, Hayakawa noted, "It's ours; we stole it fair and square."

8. In fact, the bumper guards on Cadillacs were referred to—within the General Motors styling section, at least—as "Dagmars," in acknowledgment of their resemblance to a well-endowed television starlet of the day.

9. Except for the series names—Ranger, Pacer, Corsair, and Citation—which were, of course, chosen from the finalists of those names researched. No one, however, has ever blamed the series names for the failure of the Edsel.

10. Holls interview, author's collection.

11. Brooks, p. 60.

12. Richard Stout, in an interview with the author, suspected that a separate Continental Division (with a separate engineering department) was created to keep it out from under the control of Earle MacPherson, the company's empire-building chief engineer. If so, the situation is even sillier. William Clay Ford, the youngest of the Ford brothers, was head of the Continental Division, and this was at a time when the company was still privately held by the Ford family. If Bill Ford was afraid of MacPherson, it speaks volumes about the evolving situation in Ford Motor Company.

13. *Special-Interest Autos*, Nov–Dec, 1973, p. 12.

EPILOGUE

1. Ford Motor Company papers, author's collection.

2. *Special-Interest Autos*, Nov–Dec, 1973, p. 10.

3. Ibid., p. 12. Warnock apparently was referring to the 1970 Pontiac, which many old Edsel hands insisted they had trouble telling apart from a 1958 Edsel from a distance.

4. Studebaker-Packard papers, author's collection.

5. Ford Motor Company papers, author's collection.

6. See comment above in the notes to Chapter Twelve regarding William Clay Ford and the Continental Division.

7. Stout interview, author's collection.

8. Complete with "body counts" and other cost/benefit analysis methods of measuring the success of the war effort.

9. Thomas interview, author's collection.

Bibliography

PRIMARY SOURCES

Annual Reports, Brochures, and Miscellaneous Publications

American Motors Corporation. Detroit, Michigan.
Chrysler Corporation. Highland Park, Michigan.
Ford Motor Company. Detroit, Michigan.
General Motors Corporation. Detroit, Michigan.
Hudson Motor Car Company. Detroit, Michigan.
Nash Motors Company. Detroit, Michigan.
Nash-Kelvinator Corporation. Detroit, Michigan.
Packard Motor Car Company. Detroit, Michigan.
Studebaker Corporation (Delaware). South Bend, Indiana.
Studebaker-Packard Corporation. Detroit, Michigan, and South Bend, Indiana.
Studebaker-Worthington CorporationNew York, New York.

Archives

Detroit Public Library, Automotive History Collection.
Ford Archives, Henry Ford Museum
Studebaker-Packard Papers, George Arents Research Library, Syracuse University. Syracuse, New York.
Western Reserve Historical Society, Cleveland, Ohio.

Books

Bennett, Harry. *We Never Called Him Henry*. New York, 1951.
Chrysler, Walter P., and Boyden Sparks. *Life of an American Workman*. New York, 1937.
Forbes, B. C., and O. D. Foster. *Automotive Giants of America*. New York, 1926.

MacManus, Theodore, F., and Norman Beasely. *Men, Money and Motors*. New York,
        1929.
    Pfau, Hugo. *The Custom Body Era*. New York, 1970.
    Sloan, Alfred P. *Adventures of a White-Collar Man*. New York, 1941.
    Sloan, Alfred P., Jr. *My Years With General Motors*. Garden City, New York, 1964.
    Sorensen, Charles E. *My Forty Years With Ford*. New York, 1956.
    Stout, Richard H. *Make 'Em Shout Hooray!* New York, 1988.

Interviews

By the author with John Conde, Charles Jordan, Mark Gjovic, E. T. "Bob"
Gregorie, David Holls, Semon E. Knudsen, Holden Koto, Richard Stout, Richard
Teague, Rich Thomas, and members of the original Edsel design teams in
cooperation with Robert Weenick, including Roy Brown, Jr.; Bob Jones; Gary
Griffiths and others.

Periodicals

Action Era Vehicle, Advertising Age, American Way, Argosy, Autocar (G.B.), *Auto Age,
Automobile Quarterly, Automobile Show, Automobile, Automotive Industries,
Automotive News, Automobile Topics, AutoWeek, Boston Globe, Branham Automobile
Reference Book* (various issues, 1918–1939), *Business Week, Car Classics, Car Craft,
Car & Driver, Car Life, CARS, Cars & Parts, Consumer Reports, Detroit News,
Esquire, Forbes, Fortune, Handbook of Gasoline Automobiles, Horseless Age,
Motor* (G.B.), *Hot Rod, Industrial Design, Mechanix Illustrated, Motor* (U.S.),
Motor Age, Motor Life, Motor Trend, Motor Trend Yearbook (1955–61), *N.A.D.A.
Used Car Guide* (various issues, 1934–67), *Newsweek, New York Times, Popular
Mechanics, Popular Science, Red Book National Used Car Market Report* (various
issues, 1934–55), *Road & Track, Scientific American, Special-Interest Autos, Sports
Car Graphic, Time, True's Automobile Yearbook* (1953–60), *Wall Street Journal,
Ward's*, and *Washington Post*.

SECONDARY SOURCES

Allen, Frederick Lewis. *The Big Change: America Transforms Itself, 1900–1950*.
    New York, 1952.
Barker, Ronald, and Anthony Harding. *Automobile Design: Great Designers and
    Their Work*. Cambridge, Massachussetts, 1970.
Beasely, Norman. *Knudsen, A Biography*. New York, 1947.
Beasely, Norman and George W. Stark. *Made in Detroit*. New York, 1957.
Bentley, John. *Oltime Steam Cars*. Greenwich, Connecticut, 1953.
Boyd, T. A. *Professional Amateur*. New York, 1957.
Brierly, Brooks T. *Auburn, Reo, Franklin and Pierce-Arrow versus Cadillac, Chrysler,
    Lincoln and Packard*. Coconut Grove, Florida, 1991.

Brinkley, David. *Washington Goes to War.* New York, 1988.

Brooks, John. *Fate of the Edsel and Other Business Adventures.* New York, 1963.

Bury, Martin H. *The Automobile Dealer.* Philadelphia, 1958.

Catton, Bruce. *The War Lords of Washington.* New York, 1948.

Chandler, Alfred D., Jr. *Giant Enterprise.* New York, 1964.

Clymer, Floyd. *Those Wonderful Old Automobiles.* New York, 1953.

Clymer, Floyd. *Treasury of Early American Automobiles, 1877–1925.* New York, 1950.

Cohn, David L. *Combustion On Wheels.* Boston, 1944.

Colins, Herbert Ridgeway. *Presidents On Wheels.* New York, 1971.

Conde, John. *American Motors Family Album.* Detroit, 1969.

Cornell Auto Publications. *Automobile Value Review.* Chicago, 1941.

Crabb, Richard. *Birth of a Giant.* New York, 1969.

Cravens, J. K. *Automobile Year Book and Buyer's Guide Illustrated.* Chicago, 1934.

Cravens, J. K. *Automobile Year Book and Buyer's Guide Illustrated.* Chicago, 1937.

Cray, Ed, *Chrome Colossus.* New York, 1980.

Drucker, Peter F. *Concept of the Corporation.* New York, 1946.

Drucker, Peter F. *The Practice of Management.* New York, 1954.

Editors of Automobile Quarterly. *The American Car Since 1775.* New York, 1971.

Georgano, G. N., ed. *The Complete Encyclopedia of Commercial Vehicles.* Osceola, Wisconsin, 1979.

Georgano, G. N. *Cars, 1886–1930.* New York, 1985.

Georgano, G. N., ed. *The Complete Encyclopedia of Motorcars: 1885 to the Present.* New York, 1973.

Glasscock, C. B. *The Gasoline Age: The Story of the Men Who Made It.* Indianapolis, 1937.

Gustin, Lawrence R. *Billy Durant, Creator of General Motors.* Grand Rapids, Michigan, 1973.

Heasley, Jerry. *The Production Figure Book for U.S. Cars.* Osceola, Wisconsin, 1977.

Hendry, Maurice. *Cadillac: The Standard of the World.* Princeton, New Jersey, 1973.

Herndon, Booton. *Ford.* New York, 1969.

Iacocca, Lido A. *Iacocca, An Autobiography.* New York, 1984.

Keats, John. *Insolent Chariots.* Philadelphia, 1958.

Kimes, Beverly R., ed. *Packard: A History of the Motorcar and the Company.* Princeton, New Jersey, 1978.

Kimes, Beverly Rae, and Henry Austin Clark, Jr. *Standard Catalog of American Cars 1805–1942.* Iola, Wisconsin, 1985.

Lacey, Robert. *Ford: The Men and the Machine.* New York, 1986.

Langworth, Richard M. *Studebaker, 1946–1966.* Osceola, Wisconsin, 1979.

Langworth, Richard M. *The Last Onslaught on Detroit.* Princeton, New Jersey, 1975.

Leland, Mrs. Wilfred C., and Mrs. Minnie Dubbs Milbrook. *Master of Precision.* Detroit, 1966.

Leslie, Stuart W. *Boss Kettering, Wizard of General Motors.* New York, 1983.

BIBLIOGRAPHY

MacMinn, Strother, and Michael Lamm. *Detroit Style, Automotive Form 1925–1950.* Detroit, 1985.

May, George S. *A Most Unique Machine.* Grand Rapids, Michigan, 1975.

May, George S. *R. E. Olds: Auto Industry Pioneer.* Grand Rapids, Michigan, 1977.

Nesbitt, Dick. *50 Years of American Automobile Design.* Chicago, 1985.

Nevins, Allan, and Frank E. Hill. *Ford: Expansion and Challenge, 1915–1932.* New York, 1957.

Nevins, Allan, and Frank E. Hill. *Ford: Decline and Rebirth, 1933–1962.* New York, 1957.

Nevins, Allan, and Frank E. Hill. *Ford: The Times the Man and the Company.* New York, 1954.

Pound, Arthur. *The Turning Wheel: The Story of General Motors Through Twenty-Five Years, 1908–1933.* Garden City, New York, 1934

Rae, John B. *The American Automobile.* Chicago, 1965.

Riggs, L. Spencer. Pace Cars of the Indy 500. Ft. Lauderdale, Florida, 1989.

Sedgwick, Michael. *Cars of the 1930s.* Cambridge, Massachusetts, 1970.

Sedgwick, Michael. *Cars of the Thirties and Forties.* New York, 1979.

Sedgwick, Michael. *Cars of the 50s and 60s.* New York, 1983.

Turnquist, Robert E. *The Packard Story.* New York, 1965.

United States Government, Federal Trade Commission. Report on Motor Vehicle Industry. Washington, D.C., 1939.

Used Car Statistical Bureau. Market Analysis Report. Boston, 1941.

Ward, James A. *The Fall of the Packard Motor Car Company.* Stanford, California, 1995.

Weisberger, Bernard A. *The Dream Maker.* New York, 1979.

Wilkie, David J., and the editors of Esquire. *American Autos and Their Makers.* New York, 1963.

Young, Clarence H., and William A. Quinn. *Foundation for Living.* New York, 1963.

Index